# WHETHER IT'S B

· Scrambled Tofu with Sauteed Vegetables
· Soy Sausage Casserole
· Mushroom Omelette with Tempeh Bacon

## LUNCH . . .

· Winter Vegetable Bisque
· "No Egg" Salad with Tofu Mayonnaise
· Spicy Soy Chili

## OR DINNER . . .

· Tofu Lasagna
· Sweet and Sour Tempeh
· "No Meat" Loaf and a slice of Peaches and Cream Pie

### *THE SOY GOURMET* IS FOR YOU . . .
### A SIMPLE DELICIOUS BEGINNING TO A
### HEALTHIER AND HAPPIER NEW WAY OF LIFE

ROBIN ROBERTSON is a professional chef and cooking teacher. She was trained in French cuisine, but left the restaurant industry when she realized that the combination of long hours, rich sauces, and red meat was seriously affecting her health. Today, she cooks and teaches her own innovative, low-fat vegetarian cuisine. She is also the author of two other Plume cookbooks, *366 Healthful Ways to Cook Tofu and Other Meat Alternatives* and *366 Simply Delicious Dairy-Free Recipes*.

ALSO BY ROBIN ROBERTSON

*366 Simply Delicious Dairy-Free Recipes*
*366 Healthful Ways to Cook Tofu and Other Meat Alternatives*

# THE SOY GOURMET

## ROBIN ROBERTSON

A PLUME BOOK

PLUME
Published by the Penguin Group
Penguin Putnam Inc., 375 Hudson Street, New York, New York 10014, U.S.A.
Penguin Books Ltd, 27 Wrights Lane, London W8 5TZ, England
Penguin Books Australia Ltd, Ringwood, Victoria, Australia
Penguin Books Canada Ltd, 10 Alcorn Avenue, Toronto, Ontario, Canada M4V 3B2
Penguin Books (N.Z.) Ltd, 182–190 Wairau Road, Auckland 10, New Zealand

Penguin Books Ltd, Registered Offices: Harmondsworth, Middlesex, England

First published by Plume, an imprint of Dutton NAL,
a member of Penguin Putnam Inc.

First Printing, July, 1998
10   9   8   7   6   5   4   3   2   1

 REGISTERED TRADEMARK—MARCA REGISTRADA

LIBRARY OF CONGRESS CATALOGING-IN-PUBLICATION DATA:

Robertson, Robin (Robin G.)
    The soy gourmet / Robin Robertson.
        p.      cm.
    Includes index.
    ISBN 0-452-27922-4 (alk. paper)
    1. Cookery (Soybeans)   2. Soyfoods.   I. Title.
TX803.S6R63    1998
641.6'5655—dc21
                                                                    97-43378
                                                                    CIP

Printed in the United States of America
Set in Palatino
Designed by Eve L. Kirch

# CONTENTS

# FOREWORD

When I worked as a professional chef during the 1980s, I used large quantities of meats, eggs, and dairy products to prepare dishes in classic cuisines such as French and Italian. The high cholesterol content of the sumptuous meals I prepared never crossed my mind as I added more cream to already rich foods, or sautéed them in butter.

In 1987, I made a dramatic change in my life when I decided to stop working in professional kitchens, and, in an effort to pursue a healthier lifestyle, became a vegetarian. Although I eliminated all meat and dairy products from my diet, I was reluctant to give up the aromas, flavors, and textures inherent in many of the classic dishes I was skilled in preparing. I eventually developed a style of cooking that offers the best of both worlds—a fusion of classic cooking techniques and menu ideas using natural meatless and dairy-free ingredients.

The results were well received by family and friends. Soon

I began teaching cooking classes to others who wanted to learn how to eat better without sacrificing flavor. Using soy products such as tofu, tempeh, and soy milk, I was able to recreate delectable sautéed dishes with creamy sauces, hearty stews, rich pasta dishes, and even delicious cheesecakes—without cholesterol.

In my cooking classes and workshops, I am now able to show how using soy products produces a double benefit: When using tofu or tempeh instead of meat or cheese, not only are you eating high-protein, cholesterol-free foods, but now, as recent scientific studies show, the cholesterol levels in the body can actually be reduced by eating soy foods.

Having lost both my parents to heart disease and stroke, I have a personal interest in helping people learn how to cook and eat properly. By using tofu, tempeh, and other soy foods in familiar and delicious recipes, it is my goal to make soy protein "eater-friendly," and to help people make permanent positive changes in their diets.

A recent medical study on soy protein's effect on menopause has resulted in such remarkable results that tofu is now being referred to as "natural estrogen." Indeed, in Japan, where soy is a dietary staple, there is no Japanese phrase for "hot flash."

Evidence indicates that eating more soy protein can have far-reaching benefits, whether you're trying to lower your cholesterol, relieve the symptoms of menopause and PMS, or reduce the risk of heart disease, cancer, and osteoporosis.

Whatever your health goals, if you want to achieve the natural benefits of soy protein, while still enjoying delicious food, then *The Soy Gourmet* is for you.

Robin Robertson

# INTRODUCTION
## Health Benefits of Soy Protein

## James W. Anderson, M.D.

Ten years ago I met Dr. David Jenkins, a world-renowned nutritionist and vegetarian, in Toronto on an academic matter, and afterward we went to a Chinese restaurant. The restaurant had about twelve different types of tofu or bean-curd items on the menu. Although David and his vegetarian friends dug in, I was at first reluctant. Nevertheless, I tried several types of tofu. I found I really enjoyed it, and subsequently I began to order tofu dishes regularly on my own. Last year my colleagues and I completed a large research project on soy protein that was published in the *New England Journal of Medicine*. Since then I have explored the use of tofu and soy protein in my own diet. My recent book, *Dr. Anderson's Antioxidant, Antiaging Health Program*, includes some tofu recipes. Last October in China I had a further chance to sample a wide variety of tofu. My wife and I now frequent a Chinese restaurant for a tofu meal, and Gay's favorite dinner for company is a tofu-vegetable stir-fry.

Nowadays I use soy protein daily and eat tofu every chance I get. I was delighted when Robin Robertson asked me to write this introduction. As I read the book, I became convinced that it will help you incorporate more health-promoting soy protein and tofu into your diet.

The regular intake of soybeans and soy protein such as tofu provides many health benefits. In countries where people obtain much of their protein intake from soybeans, the rates of heart disease, breast cancer, prostate cancer, and osteoporosis are much lower than in countries where people get most of their protein from animal sources. Let's review the effects of soy-protein intake on those at risk for these diseases.

*Heart attacks.* Heart attacks are the major cause of death in most developed countries, and rates are rapidly increasing in developing countries. In the U.S., every year approximately five million people have heart attacks, and approximately one million die from hardening of the arteries, which causes heart attacks, strokes, and circulatory problems. The total cost of coronary heart disease exceeds 120 billion dollars, the largest disease-related cost to health. While there are many contributing risk factors, such as cigarette smoking and high blood pressure, blood-cholesterol levels and its different particles are the key elements in hardening of the arteries.

Cholesterol is a waxy substance produced by animals but not by plants. The yolk of eggs gets its yellow color from its rich cholesterol content. Cholesterol from animal products circulates in the blood in fatty particles called lipoproteins. The two major lipoproteins related to cholesterol are low-density lipoproteins (LDL) and high-density lipoproteins (HDL).

LDL have a central role in hardening of the arteries. These accumulate in the walls of blood vessels, where they cause damage. The higher the blood cholesterol level, the more LDL that accumulate in the blood vessel wall where LDL are oxidized by free radicals. LDL that are oxidized by free radicals are like rusty particles that the body wants to dispose of. Oxidized LDL are ingested by tissue macrophages, which are cells the body uses to dispose of waste products. As the macrophage cells accumulate LDL, they become filled with fat. As these gluttonous cells get fatter and fatter, they coalesce to form little fatty tumors.

These tumors are the major contributor to heart attacks and strokes. As they grow, they bulge out into the blood vessel wall. When the tumors get really fat-laden they rupture, and a blood clot forms. This blood clot then blocks blood flow to the heart muscle or brain, leading to a heart attack or stroke.

How can we prevent heart attacks and strokes? Lowering blood-cholesterol and LDL levels is the primary approach. We can reduce our LDL levels by eating less meat, dairy products, eggs, and other sources of saturated fat and cholesterol.

HDL, or high-density lipoproteins, are major protectors of our blood vessels. They are called the "good guys" because they prevent hardening of the arteries. People with very high levels of HDL are protected from heart attacks and strokes. HDL prevent oxidation of LDL and also prevent LDL intake by fatty macrophage cells. We can raise our HDL levels by not smoking and by exercise.

*Soy protein lowers risk of heart attack.* Heart attacks are rare in China and Taiwan, where tofu and soy protein are eaten as major sources of protein. Recent research indicates that regular intake of soy protein protects from hardening of the arteries in several ways. First, it decreases LDL-cholesterol levels significantly. Second, it tends to increase HDL-cholesterol levels; this is rather unique since most diets with oat-bran intake or decreased saturated-fat intake significantly decrease HDL-cholesterol levels. Third, soy isoflavones, chemicals unique to soybeans, have antioxidant properties, which protect LDL from being oxidized. Fourth, these soy isoflavones have a healthy effect on blood vessels. If a blood vessel has accumulated fatty tumors, intake of soy protein rich in isoflavones can help keep blood vessels open.

My colleagues and I recently performed a detailed statistical analysis of all published research studies on the effects of soy protein in human subjects. This complicated statistical analysis, called a meta-analysis, was published in the *New England Journal of Medicine* in August 1995. This study clearly indicates the potency of soy protein in decreasing LDL cholesterol.

Thirty-eight studies, including 730 research volunteers, were analyzed. Soy-protein intake averaged 47 grams per day. In fourteen of the studies the test diets resembled a typical Western diet, while in twenty-one studies the diets were low in fat and cholesterol. In nineteen studies the soy-protein and control diets were considered to be comparable with respect to total fat intake, saturated-fat intake, cholesterol intake, and weight maintenance.

Soy-protein intake was associated with a 9.3 percent reduction in serum cholesterol and a 12.9 percent reduction in serum LDL cholesterol. Both of these decreases were statistically significant. The initial serum cholesterol level is the most important determinant of the serum cholesterol response to soy protein. We calculated the expected reduction in serum LDL cholesterol for research volunteers with initial serum cholesterol levels ranging from normal to severe. Those volunteers with normal initial levels had serum cholesterol decreases of 7.7 percent while volunteers with severe levels had serum cholesterol decreases of 24 percent.

This analysis documents that daily intake of soy protein significantly decreases serum cholesterol concentrations in adults and children. Since every 1 percent reduction in serum cholesterol decreases estimated risk of heart attack by 2 to 3 percent, this serum cholesterol reduction has the potential to reduce risk by up to 28 percent.

How does soy protein work in the body? Recent research with monkeys suggests that the soy isoflavones have an important role. Mary Anthony, Tom Clarkson, and colleagues at Bowman Gray Medical School in North Carolina have conducted at least three different studies with monkeys in which soy protein rich in soy isoflavones had a favorable effect, while soy protein from which the soy isoflavones had been extracted had a minimal impact. As in our human studies, soy protein intake decreased LDL cholesterol. These primate studies suggest that soy isoflavones account for more than 75 percent of the effects of soy protein.

*Breast Cancer.* Breast cancer is the second most common cancer in Western countries, but it occurs far less often in Third World and Asian countries. These differences seem to be related to environmental factors rather than genetic factors. Several research studies suggest that the high intake of soy protein rich in isoflavones protects from the development of breast cancer. Isoflavones inhibit a number of enzyme reactions and act as antioxidants. Genistein, a major soy iso-flavone, inhibits growth of a number of cancer cells in labo-ratory tests. Genistein also inhibits new blood vessel growth, essential for rapid growth of tumor cells.

*Osteoporosis.* Osteoporosis is a common condition affect-ing fifteen to twenty million Americans. Estrogen deficiency appears to contribute importantly to osteoporosis in post-menopausal women. Epidemiological studies indicate that vegetarian women who have higher intakes of soy protein have lower rates of osteoporosis than omnivorous women.

At the American Heart Association's annual scientific meeting recently, researchers at the Bowman Gray School of Medicine discussed the results of their experiments related to soy's effect on menopause. They concluded that regular consumption of soy protein significantly relieves the symp-toms of menopause. Similar studies at the University of Manchester in England suggest soy can reduce the frequency of hot flashes, as well. Studies indicate that these results are due to the ingredient in soy called phytoestrogen, the plant form of estrogen.

Soy protein products are widely available and can be pur-chased at most supermarkets. Soy beverages, tofu, textured soy protein, isolated soy protein, and soy flour can be used as foods or incorporated into many main dishes, baked goods, and other foods. Some isolated soy protein products have a standardized amount of Genistein and should be selected by women seeking the protective effects of soy isoflavones against breast cancer, osteoporosis, or meno-pausal symptoms. Some textured soy proteins have minimal amounts of soy isoflavones. Men and women can derive significant reductions in serum cholesterol levels through daily use of two servings of soy protein. This could include a soy beverage providing about 8 grams of soy protein and an entree providing about 15 to 20 grams of soy protein. This book can be a useful tool in helping people to achieve those goals.

# CHAPTER ONE

# The Soy Solution

Everywhere you look, it seems that someone is touting the health benefits of certain foods. One week we may read about the benefits of oat bran, and the next week carrots may be the featured healthy food. But a recent scientific study concludes that if you eat foods containing soy protein, you can actually lower your body's level of cholesterol. It is a report about a miracle food whose time has come. We know that dietary cholesterol is the gooey substance that clogs our arteries and increases our chances of heart disease and stroke. This book is about helping you lower your cholesterol, while giving you the secrets of how to cook fabulous meals using tofu and other soy-based foods.

Asian cultures have known for centuries what Westerners are only recently discovering: Tofu is good for you! But soy protein's many benefits are now further enhanced by new findings that reveal that it can also dramatically help you reduce cholesterol.

# The Study

Published in the *New England Journal of Medicine*, the study was conducted by Dr. James W. Anderson and his colleagues at the University of Kentucky in Lexington,* and it shows that consumption of between 25 to 47 grams of soy protein per day can actually reduce cholesterol levels by an average of 9.3 percent in a month in those who suffer from moderately high to high cholesterol. People with extremely high cholesterol levels had a 20 percent drop in their cholesterol. This is one of the most potent cholesterol-lowering factors yet to be discovered in the medical search for solutions to cardiovascular disease, America's number-one killer.

This study gives hope to anyone who wants to participate in their own healing, to reduce cholesterol, and also eat great meals they can prepare themselves.

## Where Does Cholesterol Come From?

If your diet is based on animal foods, you will consume an average of 800 milligrams of dietary cholesterol per day, most of which remains deposited in our bodies, especially in the arteries. This, of course, contributes to cardiovascular disease and other degenerative maladies. Since harmful cholesterol is only found in animal products and never in plants, it follows that if we switch to a more plant-based diet, we will not be consuming the vast amounts of that waxy gunk called cholesterol. We also know that some of the

*"Meta-Analysis of the Effects of Soy Protein Intake on Serum Lipids," by James W. Anderson, M.D., Bryan M. Johnstone, Ph.D., and Margaret E. Cook-Newell, M.S., R.D., *The New England Journal of Medicine*, August 3, 1995, p. 276.

best sources of protein, calcium, and other nutrients are soy-based foods, which, in addition to being delicious alternatives to animal foods, have actually been found to reduce existing cholesterol levels.

In order to make the transition to a cholesterol-reducing diet, it's important for veteran meat-eaters to gain a clear picture of the difference between a meat-based and a soy-based diet.

Here's a typical "well-balanced" animal-based meal:

| Food Item | Grams of Cholesterol |
| --- | --- |
| Grilled steak | 150 |
| Potato with sour cream | 42 |
| Broccoli with hollandaise | 363 |
| Roll with butter | 35 |
| Slice of cheesecake | 20 |
| Total Cholesterol = 610 grams | |

In contrast, here is a typical well-balanced soy-based meal:

| Food Item | Grams of Cholesterol |
| --- | --- |
| Grilled tempeh with onions | 0 |
| Potato with tofu sour cream | 0 |
| Steamed broccoli with lemon sauce | 0 |
| Roll with margarine | 0 |
| Slice of tofu cheesecake | 0 |
| Total cholesterol = 0 grams | |

It's important to realize that it isn't enough to say, "But I don't eat red meat anymore. Instead, I eat chicken—that's healthy, right?" The fact is, a six-ounce chicken breast contains 135 grams of cholesterol—almost as much as the 150 grams of cholesterol found in the same amount of beef!

## Amazing Benefits

Once you decide to change your health and your life by eating a delicious soy-based diet, you gain in two ways. In addition to reducing the cholesterol already present in your body, you are also *not* consuming even more of the cholesterol and saturated fat contained in the foods that created the cholesterol problem in the first place. For example, when you eat a tempeh burger or tofu cutlet instead of a hamburger or pork chop, you are not just racking up 8 to 10 grams of powerful soy protein, you are also eliminating the cholesterol and fat you would have ingested by eating the animal products.

Interestingly, it has also been discovered that consumption of soy protein lowers only the harmful cholesterol (low-density lipoprotein) without affecting the "good" cholesterol (high-density lipoprotein). Consumption of soy protein, reported Anderson's team, also reduces undesirable triglycerides.

Here's another example of how this change would work: If your favorite breakfast consists of two scrambled eggs, three strips of bacon, and toast with butter, you would be taking in approximately 458 mg. of cholesterol. However, by substituting scrambled tofu, tempeh bacon, and a miso spread, you are not only eliminating the cholesterol, but you've already begun your day with several grams of soy protein. That's what I call a real "breakfast of champions." Remember that, in addition to protein, soy products are also rich in calcium and other nutrients.

This book will show you lots of ways not only to take in beneficial amounts of soy protein, but also to make a host of delicious meals that anyone would enjoy. By using soy products in various ways throughout your day, you can discover a whole new world of cooking and dining while, at the same time, experiencing many health benefits.

Once you start going through the recipes in this book, you'll see that it's not as difficult as you may think to get your soy protein. After you familiarize yourself with tofu and other soy foods, eating them will become second nature.

## Learning to Love Tofu

One of the complaints most often heard about tofu is that, by itself, tofu is bland. The soy products that some people remember from the 1970s still make them grimace, and understandably so. But today, nearly every natural-food store and many supermarkets offer a whole new world of tofu and other soy products. The fact is that the subtle flavor of tofu is its best feature, because tofu has the ability to absorb its surroundings, whether a tangy marinade, a robust sauce, or a fruity dessert, lending itself to limitless variations. Tofu is wonderfully versatile, so don't be afraid of the mysterious white block, because it's all in how you prepare it.

## The Variety of Soy Foods

Although the most familiar form of soy protein is tofu, many other soy foods such as tempeh, miso, and soy milk are also available. Many of the recipes in this book use more than one soy product to maximize your soy protein intake. A helpful breakdown of nutrients is supplied with each recipe, which can help you determine your daily intake of soy protein. In addition, sample menus are provided to show how you can maximize your intake of soy protein without sacrificing flavor or variety. A soy foods glossary is also included in the back.

If you are under a doctor's orders to reduce cholesterol, you should consult your doctor about your plan to improve your diet as a means to lowering your cholesterol. In order to help you succeed, this book offers a plan to take the mystery out of soy foods and provides a safe and natural way to help you accomplish your health goals. The purpose of this book isn't to turn you into a vegetarian. It is simply to help you eliminate the foods that harm you and replace them with foods that will improve your health.

How can you get the needed soy protein in your diet, without having to eat tofu three times a day? With all the different kinds of soy products now available, it's easy. Just look at the soy protein levels in the following soy products:

| Soy Product | Amount of Soy Protein |
| --- | --- |
| 1 cup of soy flour | 50 grams |
| 1 cup of TSP (textured soy protein) | 22 grams |
| 1 serving soy protein powder (for shakes) | 20 grams |
| 1 soy burger | 18 grams |
| 1 cup of tofu | 16 grams |
| 1 glass of soy milk | 8 grams |
| 1 ounce soy-based "cheese" | 7 grams |

## Getting Started

A soy protein gram count per serving is provided for each recipe in this book. You may find it helpful to familiarize yourself with the average protein content of the soy foods you will be eating, decide what will work best for you, and then stop counting! When dieters count calories, it somehow makes dieting even more difficult. For this reason, I have designed a plan that can take the work out of improving your health.

The sample menus indicate the amount of soy protein contained in each meal. For example, a breakfast of scrambled tofu, tempeh bacon, and miso spread on toast contains approximately 20 grams of soy protein. If you have a dinner of lasagna made with tofu and soy cheese, and put some tofu cubes in your salad, you've just consumed about 25 grams of soy protein. If you do your own baking or make your own pasta, you may want to include soy flour as part of your ingredients to increase your soy intake even more.

One of the easiest ways to introduce soy protein into your diet is to have one delicious shake per day using one of the many soy protein powders now available. One shake alone can provide you with 20 to 28 grams of protein, especially when made with soy milk. These shakes can be enjoyed as between-meal snacks any time of day, or even as part of a meal, and will make it possible to eat just one soy-based meal per day. Since the study suggests that even 25 grams of soy protein per day can make a difference, drinking this soy shake takes the pressure off trying to count how much tofu or tempeh you've eaten each day, and will give you the opportunity to experiment with the recipes in this book to see which meals suit you best.

Since your goal is to reduce cholesterol, however, you need to replace high-cholesterol foods such as eggs, cheese, bacon, and other meats with low-cholesterol alternatives. That's where the soy foods can help, as the recipes in this book demonstrate. If you want to aggressively reduce your cholesterol, you can do so simply by combining one meal centered around soy protein with one soy shake per day. This will put you near the 47-gram daily maximum used in Dr. Anderson's study.

## How to Use This Book

In order to aid you in your meal planning, the book is organized into mealtime sections. The "Breakfasts" section includes recipes for scrambled tofu, pancakes, tofu omelets, and French toast. The "Lunches" chapter features hearty sandwiches, creamy soups, and a zesty chili. The "Dinners" section provides recipes for many tempting entrées, such as lasagna, stroganoff, cutlets, and stir-fries that everyone will enjoy. There is also a special dessert section brimming with luscious puddings, pies, and tofu cheesecakes. Receiving your desired amounts of soy protein, then, is simply a matter of making combinations, and using the soy protein gram count supplied with each recipe.*

Plan your day's meals in menu combinations that you design yourself, or consult the menu-planning suggestions on page 175, which have been designed to give you between 15 and 24 grams of soy protein per meal. By including at least one soy-based meal per day, you will easily be able to accomplish your desired soy-protein goals. When you do eat other foods, you should stay away from foods that are high in cholesterol so you're not working against these goals.

*In some recipes, a range is given for the serving size (2 to 4 servings, for example). The nutritional analysis is based on the smaller amount.

## Getting into the Habit

It is my hope that you are beginning to see how easy it can be to approach the amount of soy protein per day that is recommended for reducing cholesterol, since even 25 grams per day are shown to be helpful. That's all the more reason not to be a rigid gram counter. Just get into the habit of having soy foods for at least one meal every day, and healthful, cholesterol-free eating will become second nature. Make your own decision as to whether you want to have soy protein once, twice, or more each day. The key is to not think of this as a "diet," but merely as a positive lifestyle change in which you are simply introducing wonderful new ingredients into your meals, and improving your health.

# CHAPTER TWO

# Soy *What*?

The versatile soybean has been proven to be one of humanity's greatest nutritional treasures, owing to its abundance of protein, essential amino acids, and other nutrients, as well as its amazing versatility. While soybeans can be cooked and used as other beans, they are more likely to be found as one of the wide variety of soy products that can be made from the beans. In fact, with twelve thousand soy products available, it is reported that the retail soy foods market is a billion-dollar industry in the United States. The many types of soy foods that can be derived from soybeans include tofu, tempeh, miso, and tamari. While there is a soy foods glossary at the back of this book, the following is a more comprehensive look at these marvelous soy products, with information on where to find them, and how to store and use them.

## Soybeans

If you eat fresh-grown soybeans, you're enjoying a real treat. However, most people must procure soybeans dried, and like other dried beans, soybeans require overnight soaking. Furthermore, they take about two hours to cook. These longer-cooking beans are best used in chilis, stews, casseroles, and other slow-cooked dishes where the flavors can mingle. In the interest of presenting recipes that are easily incorporated into your existing diet, I have opted not to include any recipes calling for dried soybeans in this book. Instead, the recipes rely on the convenient and easy-to-use products made from soybeans that are quick-cooking and simple to prepare.

## Tofu

Called "meat without the bone" in China, tofu is a supple white curd, made in a process in which soybeans are cooked, ground, and then strained. The freshly strained soy "milk" is then curdled with a natural coagulant found in sea salt.

Tofu is sold in natural-food stores in a variety of textures. In recent years, tofu has grown in popularity to the point where it is now also readily available in most supermarkets. It can be found in regular or low-fat versions, and is available plain, flavored, marinated, or baked.

The bland flavor of plain tofu actually makes it extremely versatile. This protein- and calcium-rich food lends itself to all sorts of sauces, marinades, and seasonings. It can be used to make a wide diversity of dishes from soups to sauces, and entrees to desserts.

Easy to digest, tofu is high in protein, low in fat, and

contains no cholesterol. Both regular and silken varieties come in various textures such as soft, medium, firm, and extra-firm. The firm styles have had more water removed, which makes them hold together well and stand up to handling. The firm and extra-firm varieties are best for stir-fries, grilling, or sautéing, and can also be used in lasagna, sandwich fillings, and for marinated and pan-fried dishes. The soft and "silken" types of tofu are best for blending, mashing, or puréeing into creamy sauces, dressings, dips, and cheesecakes, because they can be easily blended into a smooth, pourable texture. Before tofu is added to a recipe, it should be drained and blotted to remove excess liquid.

If you do not use an entire block of tofu in a recipe, immerse the remaining tofu in cold water, and store covered in the refrigerator; change the water daily. Tofu will stay fresh for up to one week if stored in this manner.

Another way to store tofu is to drain it, wrap it, and freeze it. Bear in mind that this will alter its texture after it is defrosted, making the tofu more spongy. It also becomes more porous, and better able to soak up the flavors of marinades and sauces. Tofu defrosts quickly and needs to have the excess water squeezed out before it is used. Since freezing tofu makes it more crumbly, it's ideal for use in burgers, spaghetti sauce, or chili.

## Tempeh

Tempeh, which is another versatile meat alternative, is made by fermenting soybeans and pressing them into cakes. A wonderful source of protein, iron, and vitamins B-12 and

E, tempeh is usually found in the freezer cases at natural-food stores, sold in 8- to 10-ounce slabs. It is often blended with other beans, grains, or flavorings, which can add subtle variations in flavor, or not-so-subtle variations such as jalapeño-flavored tempeh. Tempeh's distinctive flavor and texture lends itself to more hearty and assertive dishes such as sweet-and-sour tempeh or tempeh with sauerkraut. It also stands up well to hot and spicy or highly seasoned dishes such as curries.

In order to prepare commercially made tempeh, it's best to simmer it in water for about ten minutes before using it in a recipe, to mellow out the flavor and to make it more easily digestible. After precooking it in this way, tempeh can be used to make a variety of delicious entrees as well as a great sandwich filling that looks and tastes a lot like chicken salad. There are also tempeh burgers and tempeh bacon available which are very appetizing, and which can help satisfy any cravings for something "meaty."

## Textured Soy Protein

Often called textured vegetable protein or TVP, this dried, granular product is made from soy flour and, when rehydrated, has a texture similar to ground beef. Textured soy protein is used as an extender in many common food items, and is the main ingredient of most of the commercial veggie burgers on the market. It is an excellent source of soy protein, since one cup contains 22 grams. Textured soy protein is especially good when used to make chili, spaghetti sauce, tacos, or any recipe calling for ground meat.

## Soy Milk

Low in saturated fat and free of cholesterol and lactose, soy milk makes an ideal substitute for dairy milk, and it can be used in much the same way. Pour it on your cereal in the morning, use it in baking, or use it to make creamy soups and sauces. Soy milk is sold in natural-food stores and supermarkets, and is available in low-fat and regular versions. It also comes in a variety of flavors, from plain to chocolate or vanilla. As the various brands vary slightly in both taste and texture, experiment with brands until you find the one you like best, and that affords the highest protein content. Available in aseptic containers, soymilk can be stored unrefrigerated, unopened, for several months. Once open, however, it will keep refrigerated for up to five days. Soy milk is also available in a powdered form, which can be reconstituted with water. While more economical than soy milk sold in aseptic containers, I find that it's not as flavorful, and I generally use the powdered variety solely for baking.

## Miso

Miso, the fermented soybean paste, is a staple of Japanese cuisine, and is prized for its healing properties. It has been reported to strengthen the immune system with regular use, and is a staple food of macrobiotics. Miso has a highly concentrated, salty flavor, so a little goes a long way to flavor soups and sauces, or to use in spreads. Miso is generally made from a combination of soy and various grains, such as rice or barley, which give variety in color and flavor to the various miso pastes. Miso can be found in natural-food stores as well as Asian grocery stores.

## Soy Sauce

Most of the soy sauces found in the supermarket should be avoided as they usually contain corn syrup, artificial coloring, excess salt, and other additives. Instead, go to a natural-food store and find a good tamari soy sauce that has no additives or preservatives. "Wheat-free" tamari is also available, and is desirable for anyone who has an allergy to wheat. Low-sodium tamari helps to cut down on the high sodium content common to soy sauces, and has a full, rich flavor similar to regular tamari. While not significantly high in soy protein, tamari soy sauce is a flavorful and indispensable seasoning.

## Soy Flour

Soy flour can be a boon to bakers trying to increase their soy protein, since a half cup can contain 24 grams of protein. However, it should be used to replace only about 25 percent of the flour in a recipe, since using more can create a heavy texture. Soy flour can be used as is or lightly toasted to bring out its nutty flavor.

## Dry-Roasted Soybeans

Dry-roasted soybeans or soy "nuts" are available in many natural-food stores, and may be used in the same way as any salted nut. They should be kept in an airtight container, and can be used as is for snacking, or may be ground and added to baked goods. Like most nuts, dry-roasted soybeans are high in calories, but the good news is that there are 34 grams of protein in just one-half cup.

## Soy Convenience Foods

Many varieties of products high in soy protein can be found in your natural grocer's refrigerator and freezer case in the form of hot dogs, burgers, sausages, and even cold cuts. Soy cheeses are abundant, including everything from soy mozzarella to soy cheddar and soy parmesan. When there's no time to cook, you can find a variety of frozen entrees, including tofu ravioli, tofu lasagna, and even frozen pizzas topped with soy cheese. Delicious tofu ice creams are also available in a variety of flavors.

Other convenience products include a line of tofu "helpers," not unlike those made to be used with hamburger, for creating stroganoff and curries, as well as seasoning packets which can turn a block of tofu into a sensational sandwich filling, entree, dip, or dessert.

Above all, don't be afraid to experiment. If you have a favorite recipe that calls for a meat or dairy product, try substituting a soy food product instead. A simple change would be substituting soy milk for dairy milk on your cereal. But there are other simple substitutes as well. For example, instead of using ground meat in your spaghetti sauce, use textured soy protein instead. Prepared burgers made with soy protein can provide a quick-fix alternative to a hamburger, but can also be chopped or crumbled to use in recipes calling for ground beef.

# Egg Replacers

Since eggs are the single highest source of cholesterol, I feel it is important to talk about egg replacers. Soft tofu can be used in baking and in other recipes to replace eggs, in a ratio of one-quarter cup of tofu to two eggs. As the recipes in the breakfast section of this book will attest, tofu can also make a tasty substitute for egg dishes themselves.

There are also non-soy food egg replacers that are important to note. Among them is a commercially available product made primarily from potato starch that works quite well in baking. It is called Ener-G Egg Replacer. Flaxseed is also a wonderful substitute for eggs in baking. It is first ground in a blender and then water is added. Generally speaking, when eggs are present in a recipe mainly for moisture, they can be replaced with just about any other complementary moist ingredient, such as applesauce or even water.

The health benefits of cooking with soy protein are important not just for those trying to reduce cholesterol, but for every member of the family, to begin healthy eating habits before a health problem develops. There's no better way to get someone eating right than to prepare delicious home-cooked meals for them. The easy recipes and practical hints in this book will help you achieve these goals.

# CHAPTER THREE

# Making Soy Protein Work for You

Armed with a newfound awareness of the health benefits of eating soy protein and a book full of new recipes, you are ready to begin. But where to start? This, of course, will depend on your individual and family situation, how serious you are about making a change, how quickly you want to see results, and other factors. As I mentioned earlier, you can increase your soy protein intake with as little effort as a soy protein shake once a day. But if you're washing down a bacon cheeseburger with that soy shake, it's not going to make much of an impact on improving your health.

So you should first make up your mind that there is no room for high-cholesterol foods in your life. Work on cutting down or eliminating the animal products in your diet. It can be easier than you may think. And don't worry that you won't be getting enough protein. That is a myth. The truth is that most Americans eat more protein than they need. Besides, as you'll see in the nutritional data included with the recipes in this book, protein is found in abundance in a plant-based diet, and especially in soy foods. In addition to soy foods, however, it's also important that you make room in your diet for lots of whole-grain foods and fresh vegetables each day as an overall routine of healthier eating.

Learn a few basic recipes that will become the foundation of your diet, much in the way your favorite hamburger, chicken, and pork recipes may have been in the past. It will give you something to start with and to build from for your daily menu. Especially in the transitional stages, while you're learning how to cook with tofu and other soy foods, you may want to rely more on the soy convenience foods to help wean yourself off the meat and dairy products.

For example, instead of meats, you now have tofu, tempeh, and textured soy protein to build your menus around. Since you don't want to have to eat them the same way every time, I suggest that you develop a repertoire of recipes using these basic ingredients that you can simply rotate every couple of days for variety.

Don't make drastic changes. By that I mean if you're used to eating burgers, casseroles, stews, and pasta dishes, then keep eating them. Just change some of the ingredients.

You may be pleasantly surprised to find that most soy foods are amazingly quick cooking. Where a beef stew may need to simmer for a couple hours until the meat is tender, the same stew made with tempeh or tofu is ready as soon as the vegetables are softened. If your favorite meals include meaty cutlets smothered in onions and brown gravy, you can still enjoy such a dinner using soy foods. Do you like Italian food? Try sautéing firm slices of tofu and then baking them with some tomato sauce and soy cheese, and serve with a side of pasta and a salad.

One of the easiest ways to begin to develop a taste for soy protein is by using some of the soy protein products to replace others that are high in cholesterol. Switch to soy milk for cereals, enjoy tofu ice cream instead of dairy ice cream, and try some of the tofu hot dogs, sausages, and cold cuts for a few effortless improvements to your diet that do not involve learning how to cook new recipes. Then make a plan to try one new recipe per day. Most of the recipes in this book are as simple or even easier than non-soy versions of similar recipes.

Make a menu outline at the beginning of each week before you go grocery shopping. This way, you can itemize your grocery list based on the menu plan after you check your cupboards to see what is on hand. When you first begin, a few of your new ingredients may already be on hand, but this is a good way to begin building your inventory.

## Make a List

Begin by making a list of your typical meals for a week. Taking the time to write out your usual daily menus will make it easier to pinpoint which meals need some alteration and which ones can remain the same. After listing your old menus, make another list of some specific new dishes that you will want to begin substituting. Do this gradually, in order to avoid being inundated by what may seem like a wave of new and unfamiliar ingredients and recipes. If you start out focused, it will greatly insure your success. Soon you will be able to recreate your favorite menus using the new, healthful ingredients.

When I first began to make my lists, I was surprised to discover that breakfast and lunch wouldn't have to change that much. I wrote out my old breakfast menu items on paper, listing the ingredients that I knew I wanted to eliminate, such as butter and milk. Then I listed the new ingredients that I wanted to introduce, such as soy milk and apple butter. Overall, I found that this helped me see the big picture, and cut the job down to size.

Since my former breakfast usually consisted of cereal and toast, and not bacon and eggs, it was relatively simple, but, as you will see, there is an alternative for just about every ingredient. By switching from butter to a light spread of a nut or apple butter, I enjoyed even more flavor and nutrition for my calories instead of just butterfat to clog my arteries. Though generally nondairy, many margarines are full of chemicals and fat. However, you'll probably want to buy a good-quality chemical-free margarine at a natural-food store to keep on hand for occasional use when only "butter" will do.

My former lunches often consisted of soup and a sandwich, which are simple to prepare in a variety of ways using soy protein. The simplest way to increase the amount of soy protein at lunch is to add some cubed baked or marinated tofu to your soup or salad. I find it saves lots of time to make extra food for dinner the night before, and put some aside to have for lunch the next day.

Dinners may present the biggest challenge, since that meal is often prepared for other family members who may not share your zeal for improving your health. But, as my husband says, "Make it taste good, and I'll eat it." This seems like a reasonable enough request, and hopefully you'll feel confident enough to discover that the recipes in this book will do just that.

## What Do Americans Eat?

Let's examine the typical dinner menus of many American families. Most menus include such items as barbecued chicken, hamburgers, spaghetti with meat sauce, stir-fried beef, and chili. These dishes are popular because they are delicious and economical. But you really don't have to do without these favorites—you can simply substitute ingredients. For example, instead of barbecued chicken, try barbecuing the chickenlike texture of tempeh. Your burger, formerly made of ground meat, is now made with soy protein. The trimmings don't change at all. You can still enjoy your spaghetti and chili, you're just using textured vegetable protein instead of beef. Instead of stir-frying pork or beef with your vegetables and rice, you can now use tofu or tempeh.

## Menu Planning

If you plan your meals a week in advance, it makes creating your grocery list easier, and also helps you organize your time. Menu planning is also a good tool for keeping your meals varied and interesting, and can serve as a cross-check to be sure you are eating a well-balanced diet.

Breakfasts, for example, especially in the beginning, should be something simple that you can enjoy, such as cereal with soy milk and toast. You may want to save some of the more elaborate breakfast ideas for weekend mornings when you can give the preparation the time it deserves. What I recommend is a gradual change in any type of eating behavior. That is, if you're used to eating a big breakfast of scrambled eggs, sausage, toast, and jelly, then keep doing it for now. Just establish a plan for substituting the objectionable ingredients. Indulge your cravings, but begin making your transition with a plan. And bask in the knowledge that you are ridding yourself of all that cholesterol, animal fat, and chemicals.

## So, What's for Dinner?

Eating well doesn't have to mean slaving over a hot stove. There are several convenience foods that are made from natural ingredients that can give even the most ardent cook an occasional night off. There is a wealth of frozen and packaged foods in the natural-food store for you to explore. You can find soy-cheese pizza, and various frozen entrees, from pot pies to lasagna to casseroles.

Go on a convenience-food scavenger hunt at your natural-food store. Choose a day when you will have enough time to read labels and compare products. But a word of caution: Just because you find something in a health-food store doesn't automatically mean it's good for you. Be defensive—read the labels and check ingredients with the same self-defensive scrutiny that you would use in a regular grocery store. You'll soon find products that you can trust and enjoy. You may find it a help to let the new natural convenience foods work for you, especially in the beginning.

I especially encourage you to try tofu burgers and other frozen soy protein patties from the freezer case. Combined with a whole-grain roll and all the rest of the trimmings, these burgers rival anything that can be made from ground meat. They are quick, appetizing, and enjoyable, as are tofu hot dogs, especially when slathered with a spicy mustard and a dab of vegetarian chili, sauerkraut, or cole slaw.

The frozen pizza products in the natural-food stores are made with soy mozzarella and whole-wheat crust. Or you could make your own pizza from scratch at home, using soy cheese. Either choice is better for you than traditional pizza, and your body will thank you for making the switch.

I used to sprinkle grated Romano cheese liberally over just about any Italian food. My cheese shaker now contains go-masio, a blend of ground sesame seeds and sea salt, which adds the saltiness I used to get from the cheese, and a flavorful nuttiness from the sesame seeds. Very rich in calcium, go-masio can be used to enhance Italian dishes, as well as grain and vegetable dishes and just about anything else. You can buy it ready-made or make it yourself. There is also a tasty dairy-free Parmesan available in natural-food stores. Where cheese is concerned, I learned how versatile tofu and soy milk can be as dairy substitutes in such favorite recipes as pasta primavera, lasagna, macaroni and cheese, cream soups, and cheesecakes.

When there's no time to cook, veggie burgers and other convenience foods have saved many a near-crisis dinner in my house. The idea is not to rely on convenience foods but to have them handy. These shortcuts are tools to keep us from "falling off the wagon" of healthy eating. In a weak moment, not having tofu in the house may be enough of an excuse for you to order a pepperoni pizza.

## Cravings

The trick to satisfying cravings is to use a similar type of food—with better ingredients. As already mentioned, enjoy some tofu "ice cream" when you crave dairy ice cream. If a meat craving comes along, you can quell it with something you can "sink your teeth into" like a veggie burger with fried onions or maybe some grilled tempeh with brown gravy.

Dairy cravings are usually satisfied with something made with creamy tofu, whether it be a sweet or savory dairy craving. And if you just feel like snacking, roasted soy "nuts" make a great snack and add lots of soy protein to your diet. (Alas, like many snacks, they are not low in calories!) I also like to crush soy nuts to use as a casserole topping, or to sprinkle on tofu ice cream.

As your body begins to cleanse itself of toxins, fat, and mucous, these cravings will lessen and your own feelings of good health will serve as a positive reinforcement.

I recommend that you begin familiarizing yourself with the new ingredients by introducing one new dish at a time to your table, and by making substitutions in familiar recipes so that they contain no meat or dairy. You can adjust the time for each step to your particular needs, but it's best to be patient, both with yourself and your family. This gentle approach, however, should take the sting out of making the transition. One other tip: Don't expect your new soy foods to taste exactly like meat and dairy, because they aren't exactly the same. However, they taste great in their own right, and have the added advantage of improving your health rather than damaging it. Over time, you will forget what the meat products tasted like. If you're like me, you'll lose your taste for them.

## Keeping a Journal

It may help you to keep a notebook. Use it as a journal to work up menu plans, note comments about new foods, and record how you're feeling with the new dietary changes. This is a good place to keep your recipes in order, especially any new conversion recipes that you have created from old favorites and other recipes that you find from various sources.

You can carry the list concept a step further with pages that list "soup ideas," "sandwich ideas," or a list of "easy-to-convert" recipes, such as shish kebabs, BLT's, and chili, so you have a ready supply at your fingertips when trying to conjure up new menus.

## Eating Out

Eating in restaurants doesn't have to mean forsaking soy protein. Instead, it can be an opportunity to experience exotic new ways of preparing it, since there is a wealth of delicious tofu dishes to be found on the menus of many Asian restaurants. Most Chinese restaurants have a delicious family-style bean curd as well as a Szechwan bean curd, for those who like it hot. Japanese menus often include tofu appetizers and miso soup with cubed tofu. Try Thai for a taste treat ranging from a mild sweet-and-sour tofu to incredible tofu curries that range from simply spicy to inferno-level hot. In addition, you will find tofu on many Indian and Vietnamese menus, prepared with amazing spices and wonderful herbs such as lemon grass and cilantro. Some fast-food chains are even including veggie burgers on their menus, and don't forget natural-food cafes for great soups, sandwiches, entrees, and tempting desserts.

If you find yourself in a regular restaurant, don't panic, simply adapt. Try to make wise choices by not ordering foods known to be high in cholesterol. In other words, stay away from meats, cheeses, egg dishes, and cream sauces. Try a stir-fried vegetable dish, pasta with marinara sauce, or maybe some broiled fish cooked without butter.

For extended travel, I usually bring along a few items from home, such as individual aseptic containers of soy milk which I can bring discreetly into restaurants for use on cereals. If you have a refrigerator in your hotel room, a container of tofu spread or some marinated baked tofu are good choices to keep on hand. Just do the best you can. The important thing is to relax and enjoy yourself, since exercise and stress reduction are also important factors in reducing your cholesterol.

# CHAPTER FOUR

# Breakfasts

It is said that breakfast is the most important meal of the day. It is easy to understand why when you consider that the body needs fuel to start a new day. However, many of the foods most high in cholesterol are found at breakfast. Greasy bacon, fatty sausage, and eggs, the single highest source of cholesterol, top the list. Add to this list the butter on your toast and the cream in your coffee, and we're talking about a lot of cholesterol. Do you hate to give it up? The fact is that you don't actually have to—not exactly. Just try some of the new, more healthful versions of these familiar breakfast foods.

Whether you try the soy sausage and scrambled tofu or the breakfast bread pudding, one taste will tell you that staying healthy doesn't have to mean going hungry. These recipes also make delicious lunch or light supper fare. If you're just not a "breakfast person," then turn to the chapter on shakes and whip up one of the tasty breakfast shakes. You'll enjoy the rich flavors and the feeling of increased stamina and energy, while receiving nearly 20 grams of soy protein each time you drink one.

# Scrambled Tofu with Sautéed Vegetables

*The colorful vegetables are the perfect complement to the scrambled tofu. To reduce fat intake, omit the oil and use vegetable cooking spray on a nonstick pan.*

- 1 tablespoon safflower oil
- 1 pound firm tofu, squeezed and crumbled
- 1/2 teaspoon salt, or less, to taste
- 1/8 teaspoon turmeric
- 1 medium onion, minced
- 1/2 red bell pepper, chopped
- 1/2 cup sliced mushrooms
- 1/8 teaspoon freshly ground pepper

Heat 1/2 tablespoon of the oil in a large skillet over medium heat. Add the tofu, 1/4 teaspoon of the salt, and the turmeric and cook, stirring until well mixed and heated through, about 2 minutes. Adjust the seasonings, and continue cooking over very low heat until all the liquid is absorbed. Meanwhile, prepare the vegetable topping. Heat the remaining 1/2 tablespoon oil in a medium skillet over medium-high heat. Add the onion and bell pepper, and cook until tender, about 5 minutes. Add the mushrooms, the remaining 1/4 teaspoon of salt, and the pepper, and cook 1 minute longer, or until the liquid is absorbed.

To serve, divide the scrambled tofu among serving plates and top each with a spoonful of the sautéed vegetables.

*4 servings*

## Nutritional Analysis

| | | |
|---|---:|---|
| Kilocalories | 167 | Kc |
| Protein | 12.1 | Gm |
| from soy | 11.3 | Gm |
| Fat | 10 | Gm |
| Percent of calories from fat | 53 | % |
| Cholesterol | 0 | mg |
| Dietary fiber | 1 | Gm |
| Sodium | 305 | mg |
| Calcium | 199 | mg |

# Mushroom "Cheese" Omelet

*Serve with home-fried potatoes and soy sausage or tempeh bacon for a hearty, protein-packed meal.*

|     |                                           |
| --- | ----------------------------------------- |
| 1   | tablespoon safflower oil                  |
| 1/4 | cup minced onion                          |
| 1   | cup sliced mushrooms                      |
| 1   | pound medium tofu, squeezed and patted dry |
| 1/8 | teaspoon turmeric                         |
| 1/2 | teaspoon salt, or less, to taste          |
| 1/8 | teaspoon freshly ground pepper            |
| 1/4 | cup shredded soy mozzarella               |
| 1   | tablespoon minced fresh parsley           |

Heat the oil in a large sauté pan over medium heat. Add the onion and cook until softened, about 5 minutes. Add the mushrooms and cook, stirring occasionally, until they release their liquid. Continue cooking until the liquid is reabsorbed. Add the tofu, sprinkle with the turmeric, salt, and pepper, and cook for 3 to 5 minutes, stirring occasionally, until the tofu is heated through and the liquid is absorbed.

To serve, divide the hot tofu mixture among four serving plates and pat into an omelet-shaped crescent with a spatula. Sprinkle each portion with the shredded soy mozzarella and parsley.

*4 servings*

## Nutritional Analysis

| | | |
|---|---:|---|
| Kilocalories | 146 | Kc |
| Protein | 11.4 | Gm |
| from soy | 10.9 | Gm |
| Fat | 10 | Gm |
| Percent of calories from fat | 60 | % |
| Cholesterol | 0 | mg |
| Dietary fiber | 2 | Gm |
| Sodium | 314 | mg |
| Calcium | 156 | mg |

# Scrambled Tofu with Soy Sausage and Peppers

*For added zing, serve with hot pepper sauce or salsa.*

|     |                                                  |
| --- | ------------------------------------------------ |
| 1   | tablespoon safflower oil                         |
| 1   | small onion, chopped                             |
| 1/2 | cup chopped green or red bell pepper             |
| 1/2 | cup chopped soy sausage                          |
| 1/8 | teaspoon ground fennel seed                      |
|     | Pinch of cayenne (optional)                      |
| 1   | pound soft tofu, patted dry and crumbled         |
| 1/8 | teaspoon turmeric                                |
| 1/2 | teaspoon salt, or less, to taste                 |
| 1/8 | teaspoon freshly ground pepper                   |

Heat the oil in a large skillet over medium heat, add the onion and bell pepper, and sauté until softened, about 5 minutes. Add the soy sausage, fennel seed, and cayenne (if using), and cook until the sausage is browned. Stir in the tofu, turmeric, salt, and pepper and cook for 5 minutes, stirring occasionally, until the liquid is absorbed and the tofu is heated through.

*4 servings*

## Nutritional Analysis

| | | |
|---|---:|---|
| Kilocalories | 188 | Kc |
| Protein | 13.6 | Gm |
|   from soy | 13.1 | Gm |
| Fat | 13 | Gm |
| Percent of calories from fat | 57 | % |
| Cholesterol | 0 | mg |
| Dietary fiber | 3 | Gm |
| Sodium | 489 | mg |
| Calcium | 141 | mg |

# Savory Breakfast Bread Pudding

*For a no-fuss meal in the morning, assemble this dish the night before. Combine the ingredients in the baking dish as directed, cover, and refrigerate overnight. Bring to room temperature the next morning before baking.*

|     |                                     |
| --- | ----------------------------------- |
| 2   | tablespoons safflower oil           |
| 1½  | cups chopped onion                  |
| 1   | teaspoon minced garlic              |
| 1   | pound soft tofu, crumbled           |
| 2   | cups soy milk                       |
| ½   | cup shredded soy mozzarella         |
| 1   | tablespoon Dijon mustard            |
| ½   | teaspoon ground sage                |
| ¾   | teaspoon salt, or less, to taste    |
| ⅛   | teaspoon freshly ground pepper      |
| 6   | cups whole-grain bread cubes        |

Heat the oil in a large skillet over low heat. Add the onion, cover, and cook gently for 5 minutes. Remove the cover, add the garlic, and continue cooking 2 minutes longer, stirring occasionally. In a bowl, combine the tofu, 1 cup soy milk, soy mozzarella, mustard, sage, salt, and pepper and mix well. Blend in the onion mixture. Stir in the remaining 1 cup soy milk. Lightly oil a large shallow baking dish and place the bread in it. Pour the tofu mixture over the bread, using a fork to distribute the ingredients evenly. Allow the mixture to soak until the liquid is absorbed, about 30 minutes. Preheat the oven to 350 degrees. Bake the bread pudding 30 minutes. Increase the temperature to 375 degrees. Continue baking

until puffy and lightly browned, about 10 minutes. Allow to
stand several minutes before serving warm.

*8 servings*

### Nutritional Analysis

| | | |
|---|---:|---|
| Kilocalories | 182 | Kc |
| Protein | 10.8 | Gm |
| from soy | 8.0 | Gm |
| Fat | 10 | Gm |
| Percent of calories from fat | 46 | % |
| Cholesterol | 0 | mg |
| Dietary fiber | 5 | Gm |
| Sodium | 391 | mg |
| Calcium | 120 | mg |

# Tofu Pancakes

*Breakfast can be special any morning with these fast, easy pancakes. Top with fresh fruit and maple syrup, or add some fresh blueberries to the batter for a special taste treat.*

| | |
|---|---|
| 1¹/₂ | cups unbleached all-purpose flour |
| 2 | tablespoons sugar (or a natural sweetener) |
| 1 | tablespoon baking powder |
| ¹/₂ | teaspoon salt |
| 1¹/₂ | cups soy milk |
| ¹/₄ | cup soft silken tofu |
| 1 | tablespoon safflower oil |

In a large bowl, combine the flour, sugar, baking powder, and salt and set aside. In a food processor or blender, combine the soy milk with the tofu and oil until well blended; add to the reserved flour mixture, mixing with a few swift strokes until just smooth. Ladle the batter onto a hot, lightly oiled griddle or nonstick skillet. Cook on one side for 2 to 3 minutes, or until small bubbles appear on the top of the pancakes. Flip the pancakes with a spatula and cook 2 minutes longer, or until the second sides are browned. Keep the cooked pancakes warm in a 200-degree oven while preparing the remaining pancakes.

*4 to 6 servings*

## Nutritional Analysis

| | | |
|---|---:|---|
| Kilocalories | 264 | Kc |
| Protein | 8.1 | Gm |
|   from soy | 3.3 | Gm |
| Fat | 6 | Gm |
| Percent of calories from fat | 21 | % |
| Cholesterol | 0 | mg |
| Dietary fiber | 3 | Gm |
| Sodium | 1247 | mg |
| Calcium | 16 | mg |

# French Toast

*An old family favorite with a new twist—proof that eating for your health can also mean eating deliciously. Serve with maple syrup or fruit spread.*

- 1 cup soft silken tofu
- 1 cup vanilla soy milk
- 1 teaspoon vanilla extract
- 1/2 teaspoon sugar (or a natural sweetener)
- 1/4 teaspoon ground cinnamon
- 8 slices whole-grain bread

Combine the tofu, soy milk, vanilla, sugar, and cinnamon in a blender or food processor and process until smooth and well combined. Pour the mixture into a large shallow bowl and dip the bread in it, soaking both sides. Heat a lightly oiled griddle or skillet over medium-high heat. Add the prepared bread and cook until browned on both sides, about 5 minutes.

*4 servings*

## Nutritional Analysis

| | | |
|---|---|---|
| Kilocalories | 200 | Kc |
| Protein | 10.7 | Gm |
| from soy | 4.7 | Gm |
| Fat | 5 | Gm |
| Percent of calories from fat | 22 | % |
| Cholesterol | 0 | mg |
| Dietary fiber | 7 | Gm |
| Sodium | 371 | mg |
| Calcium | 63 | mg |

# Bananas Foster French Toast

*This special-occasion dish may taste more like dessert than breakfast, but it's high in soy protein and has no cholesterol. Use bananas that have a firm yellow skin, free of bruises. If bananas are green, allow them to ripen at room temperature.*

| | |
|---|---|
| 1 | cup vanilla soy milk |
| 1/2 | cup soft silken tofu |
| 3 | ripe bananas, peeled and sliced |
| 1/8 | teaspoon nutmeg |
| 8 | slices French bread, cut diagonally |
| 2 | tablespoons soy margarine |
| 1 | tablespoon honey or brown sugar |
| 2 | tablespoons dark rum (or 1 teaspoon rum extract) |

Combine the soy milk, tofu, 1 sliced banana, and the nutmeg in a food processor or blender and process until smooth and well combined. Pour into a large shallow bowl. Place the bread in the mixture and allow it to soak into the bread, coating both sides. Heat a lightly oiled skillet over medium-high heat. Add the prepared bread and cook until just browned on each side. Remove the French toast from the skillet and keep it warm in the oven. Meanwhile, combine the margarine and honey in a skillet over medium-high heat and stir until bubbly. Add the remaining banana slices, then carefully add the rum (or extract, if using). Sauté for a minute to cook off alcohol, then pour the sauce over the reserved French toast.

*4 servings*

## Nutritional Analysis

| | | |
|---|---:|---|
| Kilocalories | 355 | Kc |
| Protein | 9.1 | Gm |
| from soy | 3.2 | Gm |
| Fat | 10 | Gm |
| Percent of calories from fat | 24 | % |
| Cholesterol | 0 | mg |
| Dietary fiber | 4 | Gm |
| Sodium | 357 | mg |
| Calcium | 62 | mg |

# Soy-Sausage Breakfast Casserole

*A satisfying make-ahead casserole that is great for breakfast, brunch, or a light supper.*

|  |  |
|---|---|
| 2 | tablespoons safflower oil |
| 1¹/₂ | cups chopped onion |
| 1 | pound soy sausage, crumbled |
| 1 | pound soft tofu, crumbled |
| 2 | cups soy milk |
| ³/₄ | teaspoon salt, or less, to taste |
| ¹/₂ | teaspoon dried thyme |
| ¹/₄ | teaspoon ground fennel seed |
| ¹/₄ | teaspoon cayenne |
| 4 | cups whole-grain bread cubes |

Heat the oil in a large skillet over medium heat. Add the onion and cook until softened, about 5 minutes. Add the soy sausage and continue cooking until the sausage browns, about 5 minutes longer, stirring occasionally. Reserve.

In a bowl, combine the tofu, soy milk, salt, thyme, fennel seed, and cayenne and mix well. Blend in the sausage mixture. Lightly oil a large, shallow baking dish and place the bread in it. Pour the sausage mixture over the bread, using a fork to distribute evenly. Let this soak until the liquid is absorbed, about 30 minutes. Preheat the oven to 325 degrees, and bake the casserole for 45 minutes. Increase the temperature to 400 degrees. Continue baking until puffy and lightly browned, about 10 minutes. Let stand 10 minutes. Serve warm.

*8 servings*

## Nutritional Analysis

| | | |
|---|---|---|
| Kilocalories | 280 | Kc |
| Protein | 18.5 | Gm |
| from soy | 16.6 | Gm |
| Fat | 17 | Gm |
| Percent of calories from fat | 52 | % |
| Cholesterol | 0 | mg |
| Dietary fiber | 5 | Gm |
| Sodium | 823 | mg |
| Calcium | 151 | mg |

# Tempeh Bacon

*This recipe is for those who want a quick and easy way to make their own cholesterol-free bacon. It is an alternative to buying one of the commercially prepared soy or tempeh bacons available at the supermarket or natural-food store. Liquid smoke is a seasoning available in most supermarkets—it imparts a "bacony" flavor to foods.*

8   ounces tempeh
    Vegetable cooking spray
1   tablespoon safflower oil
1   teaspoon liquid smoke
2   tablespoons low-sodium tamari

Slice the tempeh into thin strips resembling bacon, about ⅛ inch thick and 1 inch wide. Spray a large skillet with the vegetable cooking spray, add the oil, and heat over a medium flame. Add the tempeh slices and fry on both sides until brown and crispy. Add the liquid smoke and tamari, being careful not to splatter. Turn the tempeh over and cook for a few seconds before serving.

*2 to 4 servings*

## Nutritional Analysis

| | | |
|---|---:|---|
| Kilocalories | 263 | Kc |
| Protein | 23.3 | Gm |
|   from soy | 23.3 | Gm |
| Fat | 11 | Gm |
| Percent of calories from fat | 36 | % |
| Cholesterol | 0 | mg |
| Dietary fiber | 8 | Gm |
| Sodium | 614 | mg |
| Calcium | 112 | mg |

# Tofruitti Bagel Spread

*A great way to start your day—with something nutritious and fast. Lavish this delicious spread on your morning toast or bagel and enjoy.*

   8   ounces silken tofu, patted dry
   2   ripe bananas, peeled and sliced
   2   tablespoons fruit-sweetened peach spread
   1   teaspoon vanilla extract
   1/2 teaspoon ground cinnamon
   1/8 teaspoon ground nutmeg
   1/8 teaspoon ground allspice
   1   tablespoon peanut or almond butter (optional)

Place all the ingredients in a food processor or blender and process until well combined. Transfer the mixture to a bowl, cover, and refrigerate for several hours to allow the flavors to develop.

*4 to 6 servings*

## Nutritional Analysis

| | | |
|---|---:|---|
| Kilocalories | 119 | Kc |
| Protein | 5.1 | Gm |
| from soy | 4.4 | Gm |
| Fat | 2 | Gm |
| Percent of calories from fat | 16 | % |
| Cholesterol | 0 | mg |
| Dietary fiber | 2 | Gm |
| Sodium | 8 | mg |
| Calcium | 104 | mg |

# Tofu Breakfast Spread

*Try this high-protein, no-cholesterol alternative to cream cheese on your toasted bagel in the morning. Enjoy it plain, or add herbs, spices, and other ingredients as your own taste dictates.*

- 8  ounces silken tofu, patted dry
- 2  tablespoons minced fresh chives
- 2  tablespoons minced fresh parsley
- 1  tablespoon safflower oil
- 1  teaspoon salt, or less, to taste
- 1  teaspoon fresh lemon juice
- 1  teaspoon dried basil, dill, or other herb (optional)
- 1/4  cup finely chopped tomato, grated carrot, or other vegetable (optional)

Place all the ingredients in a food processor and blend well to achieve a smooth consistency. Transfer the mixture to a small bowl, cover, and refrigerate for several hours to deepen the flavor.

*6 to 8 servings*

## Nutritional Analysis

| | | |
|---|---:|---|
| Kilocalories | 50 | Kc |
| Protein | 3.1 | Gm |
|    from soy | 3.0 | Gm |
| Fat | 4 | Gm |
| Percent of calories from fat | 69 | % |
| Cholesterol | 0 | mg |
| Dietary fiber | 1 | Gm |
| Sodium | 391 | mg |
| Calcium | 43 | mg |

# Miso Tahini Spread

*This creamy and flavorful spread is loaded with protein and calcium and makes a tasty change from butter or cream cheese for your morning toast or bagel. Tahini is sesame paste and is available in natural-food stores and most supermarkets.*

| | |
|---|---|
| ¹/₂ | cup tahini |
| ¹/₄ | cup miso |
| ¹/₄ | cup silken tofu, patted dry |
| 2 | tablespoons fresh lemon juice |

Place all the ingredients in a food processor or blender and process until well combined. Refrigerate the unused portions in a covered container and use as a spread on toast, bread, or crackers.

*Makes 1 cup*

### Nutritional Analysis

| | | |
|---|---|---|
| Kilocalories | 108 | Kc |
| Protein | 4.1 | Gm |
| from soy | 1.6 | Gm |
| Fat | 8 | Gm |
| Percent of calories from fat | 65 | % |
| Cholesterol | 0 | mg |
| Dietary fiber | 1 | Gm |
| Sodium | 319 | mg |
| Calcium | 39 | mg |

# CHAPTER FIVE

# Let's Do Lunch

To some people, eating lunch on the run is a way of life. Others like to sit and enjoy a large midday meal. Whatever your pleasure, this chapter is filled with great lunch ideas, from soups like Winter Vegetable Bisque to a hearty chili. There are loads of tasty sandwich recipes, from an "eggless" egg-salad sandwich to a tempeh Reuben. There are recipes for every taste, from burgers to pizza, and tacos to pasta salad, all made without cholesterol and using soy protein to help reduce existing cholesterol levels.

# Creamy Vegetable Soup

*This velvety soup can be adapted to feature whatever vegetables are plentiful and in season. To do so, simply adjust the amounts of vegetables you are using to match the amounts of the ones you are eliminating. Fresh or dried herbs may also be added as desired.*

1 tablespoon safflower oil
1 medium onion, chopped
1 medium potato, peeled and chopped
1 carrot, chopped
1 rib celery, chopped
1 cup sliced zucchini
1 cup green beans, cut into 1-inch pieces
1 clove garlic, minced
3 cups water
1 teaspoon vegetable bouillon
1 teaspoon low-sodium tamari
  Salt and freshly ground pepper to taste
2 cups soy milk
1 cup silken tofu, drained
1 tablespoon minced fresh parsley (garnish)

Heat the oil in a large saucepan over medium heat. Add the onion, potato, carrot, and celery; cover and cook, stirring occasionally, until softened, about 5 minutes. Reduce the heat to low, add the zucchini, green beans, garlic, and 3 cups water, and simmer, covered, until the vegetables are tender, about 20 minutes. Remove from the heat. Add the vegetable bouillon, tamari, and salt and pepper to taste. Working in batches, puree the soup in a food processor, blending until smooth. Transfer the mixture to a large bowl. Place the soy milk and tofu in the food processor and add about ⅓ cup of the soup mixture, processing to blend well. Slowly stir the soy milk mixture into the soup. Adjust the seasoning, and slowly reheat to desired serving temperature, being careful not to boil. Garnish with parsley.

*6 servings*

| Nutritional Analysis | | |
| --- | --- | --- |
| Kilocalories | 130 | Kc |
| Protein | 6.6 | Gm |
| from soy | 4.5 | Gm |
| Fat | 5 | Gm |
| Percent of calories from fat | 36 | % |
| Cholesterol | 0 | mg |
| Dietary fiber | 4 | Gm |
| Sodium | 234 | mg |
| Calcium | 50 | mg |

# Winter Vegetable Bisque

*Rich in color and flavor, this soup is high in protein, calcium, and beta carotene.*

- 1   tablespoon olive oil
- 1/2   cup diced onion
- 1/2   cup minced celery
- 1   medium carrot, chopped
- 1   medium potato, peeled and diced
- 1   cup peeled and diced butternut squash
- 1   teaspoon minced garlic
- 1/2   teaspoon minced fresh thyme, or 1/8 teaspoon dried
- 3   cups water
- 1   cup silken tofu, drained
- 1   cup soy milk
  - Salt and freshly ground pepper to taste

Heat the oil in a large saucepan over medium heat. Add the onion, celery, and carrot, and cook covered for 5 minutes. Add the potato, squash, garlic, thyme, and 3 cups water, and simmer 20 minutes or until the vegetables are tender. Puree the mixture in a food processor until smooth, then return it to the saucepan. Blend the tofu and soy milk in the food processor with 1/2 cup of the soup mixture. Slowly stir the tofu mixture into the soup, and add salt and pepper to taste. Heat the soup over low heat until hot, being careful not to boil.

*6 servings*

## Nutritional Analysis

| | | |
|---|---:|---|
| Kilocalories | 121 | Kc |
| Protein | 6.2 | Gm |
|    from soy | 4.4 | Gm |
| Fat | 5 | Gm |
| Percent of calories from fat | 36 | % |
| Cholesterol | 0 | mg |
| Dietary fiber | 3 | Gm |
| Sodium | 35 | mg |
| Calcium | 85 | mg |

# Tofu Miso Soup

*A light yet full-bodied soup that is excellent paired with a sandwich for a satisfying lunch.*

|   |   |
|---|---|
| 5 | cups water |
| 1/2 | cup sliced mushrooms |
| 1/4 | cup chopped scallions |
| 1/4 | cup finely shredded cabbage |
| 1/4 | cup finely shredded carrot |
| 1 | tablespoon low-sodium tamari |
| 3 | tablespoons miso paste |
| 8 | ounces firm tofu, cut into small dice |

Bring the 5 cups water to a boil, add the mushrooms, scallions, cabbage, carrot, and tamari. Reduce the heat to medium and simmer for 10 minutes, or until the vegetables soften. Reduce the heat to low. Place about 1/4 cup of the hot soup mixture in a small bowl and add the miso paste, blending well. Stir the blended miso into the soup and simmer for 2 minutes, being careful not to boil. Add the tofu, and adjust the seasonings.

*4 servings*

## Nutritional Analysis

| | | |
|---|---:|---|
| Kilocalories | 91 | Kc |
| Protein | 8.2 | Gm |
|   from soy | 7.6 | Gm |
| Fat | 3 | Gm |
| Percent of calories from fat | 30 | % |
| Cholesterol | 0 | mg |
| Dietary fiber | 1 | Gm |
| Sodium | 642 | mg |
| Calcium | 124 | mg |

# "No Egg" Salad

*If you prepare this sandwich filling ahead of time, it allows the flavors a chance to develop. Serve on toasted whole-grain bread, or stuff into pita pockets with lettuce and tomato.*

|   |   |
|---|---|
| 1 | pound firm tofu, drained and patted dry |
| 1/3 | cup Tofu Mayonnaise (recipe follows) |
| 1/4 | cup minced celery |
| 1/4 | cup minced scallion |
| 1 | dill pickle, chopped |
| 2 | tablespoons Dijon mustard |
| 1/8 | teaspoon turmeric |
| 1/2 | teaspoon salt |
| 1/8 | teaspoon cayenne |

Place the tofu in a mixing bowl and crumble with a fork. Add the remaining ingredients, blending well until thoroughly mixed. Refrigerate 30 minutes or overnight. When ready to serve, taste to adjust seasonings.

*4 servings*

## Nutritional Analysis

| | | |
|---|---:|---|
| Kilocalories | 129 | Kc |
| Protein | 13.2 | Gm |
|   from soy | 12.3 | Gm |
| Fat | 6 | Gm |
| Percent of calories from fat | 39 | % |
| Cholesterol | 0 | mg |
| Dietary fiber | 1 | Gm |
| Sodium | 617 | mg |
| Calcium | 234 | mg |

# Tofu Mayonnaise

*Make your own homemade tofu mayonnaise with this easy recipe, or try one of the commercially prepared versions, available in natural-food stores.*

| | |
|---|---|
| 1 | 12-ounce package silken tofu, drained |
| 2 | tablespoons cider vinegar |
| 1¹/₂ | tablespoons Dijon mustard |
| 1 | teaspoon sugar (or a natural sweetener) |
| ¹/₂ | teaspoon salt |
| ¹/₈ | teaspoon turmeric |
| ¹/₈ | teaspoon cayenne (optional) |

Place all the ingredients in a food processor or blender and process until smooth and well combined. Adjust seasonings. Keep refrigerated in a glass jar or other container with a tight lid.

*Makes about 2 cups*

### Nutritional Analysis

| | | |
|---|---|---|
| Kilocalories | 7 | Kc |
| Protein | .7 | Gm |
|   from soy | .7 | Gm |
| Fat | 0 | Gm |
| Percent of calories from fat | 40 | % |
| Cholesterol | 0 | mg |
| Dietary fiber | 0 | Gm |
| Sodium | 41 | mg |
| Calcium | 16 | mg |

# Tempeh Reuben Sandwich

8   ounces tempeh, cut into 1/8-inch-thick slices
1   tablespoon safflower oil
1   tablespoon soy margarine
4   slices rye bread
2   ounces soy cheese, sliced thin
4   tablespoons sauerkraut
2   tablespoons Thousand Island Dressing
      (recipe follows)

Place the tempeh in a saucepan of boiling water. Reduce the heat to low and simmer for 10 minutes. Remove the tempeh from the saucepan and allow to cool. Pat dry. Heat the oil in a large skillet over medium heat, add the tempeh, and cook until golden brown on both sides. Transfer to a plate and reserve. Spread the margarine on one side of each slice of bread. Place two of the bread slices, margarine side down, in the skillet. Layer both slices with the soy cheese, the reserved tempeh, and the sauerkraut. Top each with the remaining two slices of bread, margarine side up. Cook the sandwiches until lightly browned on both sides, turning once. Serve with the Thousand Island Dressing.

*2 sandwiches*

## Nutritional Analysis

| | | |
|---|---:|---|
| Kilocalories | 612 | Kc |
| Protein | 35.0 | Gm |
|   from soy | 29.3 | Gm |
| Fat | 30 | Gm |
| Percent of calories from fat | 42 | % |
| Cholesterol | 0 | mg |
| Dietary fiber | 14 | Gm |
| Sodium | 856 | mg |
| Calcium | 306 | mg |

# Thousand Island Dressing

*Use this easy recipe to make dressing for sandwiches, burgers, and salads.*

- 3/4 **cup tofu mayonnaise (homemade or purchased)**
- 1/4 **cup ketchup**
- 1/4 **cup sweet pickle relish**
- 1 **tablespoon minced scallion**
- 1/4 **teaspoon Tabasco sauce**
- 1/4 **teaspoon salt**
- 1/8 **teaspoon freshly ground pepper**

Combine all the ingredients in a bowl and mix until well combined. Chill before serving. Refrigerate unused portions in a covered container.

*Makes 1 cup*

| Nutritional Analysis | | |
|---|---|---|
| Kilocalories | 39 | Kc |
| Protein | 1.4 | Gm |
| from soy | 1.1 | Gm |
| Fat | 1 | Gm |
| Percent of calories from fat | 12 | % |
| Cholesterol | 0 | mg |
| Dietary fiber | 0 | Gm |
| Sodium | 350 | mg |
| Calcium | 28 | mg |

# "No Chicken" Salad

*This protein-packed alternative to chicken salad is a favorite at my house. Use as you would chicken salad: on toasted bread or bagels, stuffed into pita pockets, or scooped onto a bed of lettuce.*

|   |   |
|---|---|
| 1 | pound tempeh |
| 1 | tablespoon safflower oil |
| 1/2 | cup tofu mayonnaise (homemade or purchased) |
| 1 | tablespoon Dijon mustard |
| 1 | teaspoon fresh lemon juice |
| 1/4 | cup finely chopped scallion |
| 1/4 | cup finely chopped celery |
| 1/4 | cup finely chopped red bell pepper |
| 1 | tablespoon minced fresh parsley |
| 1 | tablespoon sweet pickle relish |
| 1/2 | teaspoon salt |
| 1/8 | teaspoon freshly ground pepper |

Place the tempeh in a saucepan of boiling water. Reduce the heat to low and allow to simmer for 10 minutes. Remove the tempeh from the pan and allow to cool. Pat dry and chop well. Heat the oil in a medium skillet over moderate heat, add the tempeh, and cook until golden brown, about 5 minutes. Allow to cool. In a bowl, combine the tempeh with the remaining ingredients and mix well to combine. Adjust seasoning.

*Makes 2 cups*

## Nutritional Analysis

| | | |
|---|---|---|
| Kilocalories | 289 | Kc |
| Protein | 23.6 | Gm |
| from soy | 22.9 | Gm |
| Fat | 13 | Gm |
| Percent of calories from fat | 38 | % |
| Cholesterol | 0 | mg |
| Dietary fiber | 9 | Gm |
| Sodium | 440 | mg |
| Calcium | 156 | mg |

# Sloppy Joes

*A favorite with children of all ages. This actually tastes even better the day after it's made, so make it the night before for a no-fuss lunch the next day. Serve on whole-grain rolls with a bowl of soup for a hot and hearty lunch or light supper.*

|       |                                                   |
|-------|---------------------------------------------------|
| 1     | tablespoon safflower oil                          |
| 1     | cup chopped onion                                 |
| 1/2   | cup chopped green or red bell pepper              |
| 2     | cups rehydrated textured soy protein              |
| 1/2   | teaspoon salt, or less, to taste                  |
| 1/8   | teaspoon freshly ground black pepper              |
| 1     | cup ketchup or tomato sauce                       |
| 1     | tablespoon sugar (or a natural sweetener)         |
| 1     | tablespoon prepared mustard                       |
| 1     | teaspoon Worcestershire sauce                     |

Heat the oil in a large skillet over medium-high heat, add the onion and bell pepper, cover, and cook about 5 minutes, or until the vegetables are soft. Remove the cover and add the textured soy protein, salt, and pepper. Cook 2 minutes, stirring occasionally. Add the remaining ingredients, and simmer for 10 minutes. Adjust seasonings.

*6 servings*

## Nutritional Analysis

| | | |
|---|---:|---|
| Kilocalories | 104 | Kc |
| Protein | 3.9 | Gm |
| from soy | 2.6 | Gm |
| Fat | 3 | Gm |
| Percent of calories from fat | 21 | % |
| Cholesterol | 0 | mg |
| Dietary fiber | 2 | Gm |
| Sodium | 648 | mg |
| Calcium | 31 | mg |

# Spicy Soy Chili

*A crumblier texture is achieved when the tofu is frozen, making it ideal for this zesty chili recipe. Textured soy protein may be substituted for the tofu and tempeh, if desired.*

| | |
|---|---|
| 2 | tablespoons olive oil |
| 1 | large onion, chopped |
| 1 | garlic clove, minced fine |
| 8 | ounces tempeh, grated |
| 1 | pound frozen firm tofu, thawed, squeezed, and crumbled |
| 1 | 8-ounce can tomato paste |
| 4 | cups hot water |
| 1 | 16-ounce can pinto beans, drained and rinsed |
| 1/4 | cup salsa |
| 2 | tablespoons chili powder |
| 1 | teaspoon salt |
| 1/4 | teaspoon freshly ground pepper |
| 1/8 | teaspoon cayenne |

Heat the oil in a large saucepan over medium heat. Add the onion and cook, covered, until softened, about 5 minutes. Remove the cover, add the garlic and tempeh, and cook, stirring, for 1 minute. Add the tofu and mix well. Add the remaining ingredients. Simmer for 1 hour, stirring occasionally.

*6 servings*

## Nutritional Analysis

| | | |
|---|---:|---|
| Kilocalories | 275 | Kc |
| Protein | 19.3 | Gm |
|   from soy | 14.4 | Gm |
| Fat | 11 | Gm |
| Percent of calories from fat | 35 | % |
| Cholesterol | 0 | mg |
| Dietary fiber | 8 | Gm |
| Sodium | 456 | mg |
| Calcium | 206 | mg |

# Creole Tempeh Cutlets

*The spicy sauce is the perfect complement to these cutlets, which can be served on toasted rolls or on a bed of rice. Either way, the extra sauce may be passed separately.*

|     |     |
| --- | --- |
| 2 | tablespoons safflower oil |
| 1/4 | cup minced green bell pepper |
| 1 | tablespoon minced celery |
| 2 | tablespoons minced scallion |
| 1 | 16-ounce can peeled tomatoes, drained and chopped fine |
| 2 | tablespoons prepared horseradish |
| 1 | tablespoon minced fresh parsley |
| 1/2 | teaspoon salt |
| 1 | teaspoon hot pepper sauce |
| 1 | pound tempeh, cut into 4-inch cutlets |

Heat 1 tablespoon of the oil in a small saucepan over medium heat. Add the bell pepper and celery and cook for 5 minutes. Add the scallion, tomatoes, horseradish, parsley, salt, and hot pepper sauce. Simmer 10 minutes, adjust seasonings, and set aside. Place the tempeh in a saucepan of boiling water. Reduce the heat to low and simmer 10 minutes. Remove the tempeh from the saucepan and pat dry. Heat the remaining 1 tablespoon oil in a large skillet over medium-high heat. Add the tempeh and cook until golden brown on both sides, about 5 minutes. Add the reserved sauce and simmer 5 minutes.

*4 servings*

## Nutritional Analysis

| | | |
|---|---:|---|
| Kilocalories | 318 | Kc |
| Protein | 23.0 | Gm |
| from soy | 21.5 | Gm |
| Fat | 16 | Gm |
| Percent of calories from fat | 42 | % |
| Cholesterol | 0 | mg |
| Dietary fiber | 10 | Gm |
| Sodium | 498 | mg |
| Calcium | 147 | mg |

# Pizza with Mushroom Topping

*The hot red pepper flakes and ground fennel add a sausagelike flavor to the sautéed mushrooms and tofu.*

1¹/₂  teaspoons active dry yeast
²/₃  cup warm water
1¹/₂  cups all-purpose flour
³/₄  teaspoon salt
3  tablespoons olive oil
1  cup tomato sauce
¹/₂  teaspoon minced fresh basil, or ¹/₄ teaspoon dried
¹/₄  teaspoon minced fresh oregano,
     or ¹/₄ teaspoon dried
4  ounces soy mozzarella, grated
1  cup sliced mushrooms
1  cup drained and crumbled firm tofu
¹/₈  teaspoon red pepper flakes
¹/₈  teaspoon ground fennel seed

Dissolve the yeast in the water. In a food processor, combine the flour and ¹/₂ teaspoon of the salt. With the machine running, pour in the dissolved yeast and pulse until the mixture is crumbly. With the machine running, add 2 tablespoons of the olive oil and mix for a few more seconds. If the dough is too moist, add an additional tablespoon of flour. Process until the dough forms a ball. Lightly oil the dough and place in a large bowl, covering it with plastic wrap and a dry towel. Set the bowl in a warm place and allow to rise until doubled in size, about 1 hour.

Preheat the oven to 450 degrees. Place the dough on a

floured surface and knead four or five times. Flatten into a circle. Using a floured rolling pin, roll out until about 12 inches across. Place the dough on a pizza pan or cookie sheet, stretching to fit if necessary. Spread the tomato sauce on top of the dough and sprinkle with the basil, oregano, and soy cheese.

To prepare the topping, heat the remaining 1 tablespoon olive oil in a medium skillet over medium-high heat. Add the mushrooms, tofu, remaining ¼ teaspoon salt, red pepper flakes, and ground fennel seed. Sauté for 2 to 3 minutes, or until the mushrooms are tender, and then spread the topping mixture evenly over the pizza. Bake for 25 to 30 minutes, or until the crust is golden brown.

*Makes one 12-inch pizza*

## Nutritional Analysis

| | | |
|---|---|---|
| Kilocalories | 282 | Kc |
| Protein | 12.9 | Gm |
| from soy | 8.4 | Gm |
| Fat | 13 | Gm |
| Percent of calories from fat | 40 | % |
| Cholesterol | 0 | mg |
| Dietary fiber | 3 | Gm |
| Sodium | 481 | mg |
| Calcium | 163 | mg |

# Soy-Good Burgers

*Serve on toasted rolls with lettuce, tomato, and all the trimmings. Grill some onions and mushrooms and top with soy cheese for extra flavor.*

| | |
|---|---|
| 1 | cup drained and crumbled firm tofu |
| 1 | cup cooked lentils, mashed |
| 1/2 | cup ground dry-roasted soybeans |
| 1/4 | cup grated onion |
| 1 | tablespoon soy flour |
| 1/4 | cup minced fresh parsley |
| 1 | teaspoon low-sodium tamari |
| 1 | teaspoon Dijon mustard |
| 1/2 | teaspoon salt |
| 1/8 | teaspoon freshly ground pepper |
| 1 | cup dry bread crumbs |
| 2 | tablespoons safflower oil |

In a large bowl, combine all the ingredients except the bread crumbs and oil. Mix the ingredients in a bowl until thoroughly combined. If too moist, add 1/4 cup of the bread crumbs. Shape the mixture into six patties. Coat with the bread crumbs. Heat the oil in a large skillet over medium heat. Cook the patties until golden brown, about 5 minutes per side.

*6 servings*

## Nutritional Analysis

| | | |
|---|---:|---|
| Kilocalories | 260 | Kc |
| Protein | 15.9 | Gm |
|   from soy | 10.4 | Gm |
| Fat | 11 | Gm |
| Percent of calories from fat | 36 | % |
| Cholesterol | 0 | mg |
| Dietary fiber | 5 | Gm |
| Sodium | 395 | mg |
| Calcium | 165 | mg |

# Tacos

*Grated tempeh may be used instead of the textured soy protein in this recipe, if you prefer.*

| | |
|---|---|
| 1 | tablespoon safflower oil |
| 1/2 | cup minced onion |
| 2 | cups reconstituted textured soy protein granules |
| 1 | cup prepared salsa |
| 1 | tablespoon tomato paste |
| | Salt and freshly ground pepper to taste |
| 8 | taco shells |
| | Toppings: grated soy cheese, shredded lettuce, and diced tomato |

Preheat the oven to 350 degrees. Heat the oil in a large skillet over medium-high heat. Add the onion, cover, and cook 5 minutes, or until the onion is soft. Remove the lid, stir in the soy granules, salsa, and tomato paste, and bring to a boil. Reduce the heat to low, season with salt and pepper to taste, and simmer for 10 minutes.

Meanwhile, heat the taco shells in the oven at 350 degrees for about 5 minutes. Spoon the hot filling into the taco shells and serve topped with soy cheese, lettuce, and tomato.

*4 servings*

## Nutritional Analysis

| | | |
|---|---|---|
| Kilocalories | 195 | Kc |
| Protein | 6.7 | Gm |
| from soy | 3.8 | Gm |
| Fat | 10 | Gm |
| Percent of calories from fat | 42 | % |
| Cholesterol | 0 | mg |
| Dietary fiber | 4 | Gm |
| Sodium | 105 | mg |
| Calcium | 72 | mg |

# Baked Marinated Tofu

*While the commercially prepared variety of baked tofu is delicious and convenient, here's a recipe you can make yourself, to eat as is or use in recipes.*

- 1/3 cup safflower oil
- 1/3 cup toasted sesame oil
- 1/3 cup cider vinegar
- 1/4 cup low-sodium tamari
- 2 teaspoons sugar (or a natural sweetener)
- 1 teaspoon minced garlic
- 1 pound firm tofu, cut into 1/2-inch-thick slices

Combine all the ingredients, except the tofu, in a small saucepan over high heat and bring to a boil. Place the tofu in a shallow baking dish. Pour the marinade over the top. Allow the tofu to marinate 30 minutes or more, turning once. Preheat the oven to 350 degrees. Bake the tofu in the oven for 10 minutes, then turn the slices over and bake 10 minutes longer. Remove the tofu from the marinade with a slotted spatula to serve.

*4 servings*

## Nutritional Analysis

| | | |
|---|---|---|
| Kilocalories | 237 | Kc |
| Protein | 12.1 | Gm |
|   from soy | 12.0 | Gm |
| Fat | 18 | Gm |
| Percent of calories from fat | 69 | % |
| Cholesterol | 0 | mg |
| Dietary fiber | 0 | Gm |
| Sodium | 240 | mg |
| Calcium | 193 | mg |

# Pasta Salad with Tofu

*Instead of plain tofu, baked marinated tofu can be used, if desired. Served on a bed of mixed greens, this colorful salad is a meal in itself.*

| | |
|---|---|
| 1 | pound rotini, or other small, shaped pasta |
| 1/2 | cup olive oil |
| 1/4 | cup cider vinegar |
| 2 | teaspoons low-sodium tamari |
| 1/2 | teaspoon sugar (or a natural sweetener) |
| 1/4 | teaspoon dry mustard |
| 1/4 | teaspoon salt |
| 11/2 | cups extra-firm tofu, cut into 1/2-inch cubes |
| 1/2 | cup sliced carrots, blanched (see note) |
| 1/2 | cup thinly sliced celery |
| 1/2 | cup frozen peas, thawed |
| 1/2 | cup halved cherry tomatoes |
| 1/4 | cup minced fresh parsley |
| 2 | tablespoons minced scallions |

Cook the pasta according to the package directions. Drain well. In a small bowl, combine the oil, vinegar, tamari, sugar, mustard, and salt, and reserve. In a large bowl, combine the cooked pasta with the remaining ingredients. Add the reserved dressing to the pasta salad, tossing to coat well. Adjust seasonings.

*6 to 8 servings*

*Note:* Blanch carrots by placing them in a pot of boiling water for about 1 minute—just long enough to soften slightly. This can also be done in a vegetable steamer. After blanching, the carrots should be plunged into cold water and drained to stop the cooking process.

### Nutritional Analysis

| | | |
|---|---|---|
| Kilocalories | 522 | Kc |
| Protein | 17.4 | Gm |
| from soy | 6.6 | Gm |
| Fat | 22 | Gm |
| Percent of calories from fat | 38 | % |
| Cholesterol | 0 | mg |
| Dietary fiber | 3 | Gm |
| Sodium | 203 | mg |
| Calcium | 138 | mg |

# Composed Salad Platter

*A striking combination of delicious salads and fresh vegetables. Baked tofu is available in the refrigerator case at most natural-food stores, or can be made using the recipe on page 80. The dressing for this salad should be made ahead of time to allow the flavors to develop.*

    4   cups torn mixed greens (romaine,
            Boston lettuce, etc.)
    1   cup prepared pasta salad (see page 82)
    1   cup prepared tempeh salad (see page 66)
    1   cup prepared tofu salad (see page 59)
    6   ounces marinated baked tofu,
            cut into ¼-inch strips
    6   cherry tomatoes
    2   radishes
  ½   cucumber
        Creamy Herb Dressing (recipe follows)

Line two dinner plates with the mixed lettuce. Mound ½ cup each of the pasta, tempeh, and tofu salads on each plate, arranging the mounds at equal distances from each other. Place the tofu strips in a spokelike arrangement between the mounds of salad, dividing them evenly. Garnish with the remaining ingredients: Slice the cherry tomatoes in half and arrange on each plate. Cut the radishes decoratively to make roses, or simply trim and place on the plates. Slice the cucumber and fan out groups of three slices on each plate. Pass the Creamy Herb Dressing separately.

*2 servings*

## Nutritional Analysis

| | | |
|---|---:|---|
| Kilocalories | 725 | Kc |
| Protein | 50.3 | Gm |
| from soy | 42.8 | Gm |
| Fat | 35 | Gm |
| Percent of calories from fat | 43 | % |
| Cholesterol | 0 | mg |
| Dietary fiber | 14 | Gm |
| Sodium | 1266 | mg |
| Calcium | 587 | mg |

# Creamy Herb Dressing

*This flavorful all-purpose dressing can be used on all your favorite salad greens, or as a dip for raw vegetables.*

|     |                                        |
| --- | -------------------------------------- |
| 1   | cup silken tofu, drained               |
| 1/4 | cup soy milk                           |
| 1   | tablespoon olive oil                   |
| 1   | tablespoon cider vinegar               |
| 2   | tablespoons chopped scallions          |
| 1   | tablespoon chopped fresh parsley       |
| 1   | teaspoon snipped fresh chives          |
| 1/2 | teaspoon dried basil                   |
| 1   | teaspoon fresh lemon juice             |
| 1   | teaspoon Dijon mustard                 |
| 1   | teaspoon low-sodium tamari             |
| 1/4 | teaspoon salt, or to taste             |
| 1/8 | teaspoon freshly ground pepper         |

Combine all the ingredients in a food processor or blender and mix until smooth. Transfer to a covered container, and refrigerate.

*Makes about 1 1/2 cups*

## Nutritional Analysis

| | | |
|---|---|---|
| Kilocalories | 25 | Kc |
| Protein | 1.3 | Gm |
| from soy | 1.2 | Gm |
| Fat | 2 | Gm |
| Percent of calories from fat | 65 | % |
| Cholesterol | 0 | mg |
| Dietary fiber | 0 | Gm |
| Sodium | 70 | mg |
| Calcium | 11 | mg |

# Salad of Mixed Greens with Creamy Mustard Dressing

*While plain tofu cubes may be used, the flavorful marinated variety, from the natural-food store or made using the recipe on page 80, is the perfect accent to the tangy dressing.*

¼  cup silken tofu, drained
¼  cup soy milk
2  tablespoons minced fresh parsley
1  tablespoon minced scallion
2  tablespoons Dijon mustard
1  tablespoon cider vinegar
   Salt and freshly ground pepper
½  small head of Boston lettuce, torn into
     bite-size pieces
½  small head of red or green leaf lettuce,
     torn into bite-size pieces
8  ounces baked marinated tofu, cut into small dice

In a food processor, combine the tofu, soy milk, parsley, scallions, mustard, vinegar, and salt and pepper to taste. Wash and spin the lettuce, and place in a serving bowl. To serve, add the tofu cubes and dressing to the lettuce, and toss to combine.

*4 servings*

## Nutritional Analysis

| | | |
|---|---|---|
| Kilocalories | 151 | Kc |
| Protein | 8.4 | Gm |
| from soy | 7.2 | Gm |
| Fat | 10 | Gm |
| Percent of calories from fat | 61 | % |
| Cholesterol | 0 | mg |
| Dietary fiber | 1 | Gm |
| Sodium | 170 | mg |
| Calcium | 142 | mg |

# Tofu-Tahini Sandwich Spread

*A tasty sandwich spread that can be thinned with soy milk and used as a dip for crudités.*

1/2  cup chopped celery
2  scallions, trimmed
2  cups firm silken tofu, drained and patted dry
1/2  cup tahini (sesame paste)
3  tablespoons fresh lemon juice
1  tablespoon Dijon mustard
2  tablespoons drained capers
1/2  cup minced fresh parsley
1  teaspoon paprika
1/2  teaspoon salt
1/8  teaspoon cayenne

Place the celery and scallions in a food processor and mince fine. Add the remaining ingredients and process until well combined. Transfer the spread to a small bowl, and refrigerate covered for at least an hour before serving to allow flavors time to develop.

*Makes about 2 1/2 cups*

## Nutritional Analysis

| | | |
|---|---:|---|
| Kilocalories | 34 | Kc |
| Protein | 2.4 | Gm |
| from soy | 1.8 | Gm |
| Fat | 2 | Gm |
| Percent of calories from fat | 51 | % |
| Cholesterol | 0 | mg |
| Dietary fiber | 0 | Gm |
| Sodium | 123 | mg |
| Calcium | 16 | mg |

# CHAPTER SIX

# What's for Dinner?

You may be wondering how you're going to answer that perennial question, now that you've decided to limit your intake of high-cholesterol foods around which many dinner ideas revolve. But you'll stop wondering once you delve into this chapter filled with over twenty tempting dinner ideas ranging from Tofu Cutlets with Creamy Mushroom Sauce to a hearty Simmered Soy Stew. No need to give up your favorites, since you can still make lasagna, macaroni and cheese, "meat" loaf, and even quiche, all using fabulous soy protein foods.

Try Sweet-and-Sour Tempeh or Curried Tofu when you feel like something exotic, or indulge in a rich and creamy helping of Tofu Stroganoff. No need to feel guilty, because not only will you be eating foods with no cholesterol, you will actually be helping lower your cholesterol at the same time.

# Tofu Lasagna

*A delicious way to get a triple helping of soy protein using tofu, TVP, and soy cheese. This make-ahead dish is guaranteed to please. Use your favorite meatless tomato sauce.*

| | |
|---|---|
| 2 | pounds firm tofu, drained and patted dry |
| 1/4 | cup minced fresh parsley |
| 3/4 | teaspoon salt |
| 1/4 | teaspoon freshly ground pepper |
| 4 | cups tomato sauce |
| 1 | pound lasagna noodles, cooked according to package directions and drained |
| 1 | cup rehydrated TVP (textured soy protein) |
| 8 | ounces soy mozzarella, shredded |

Preheat the oven to 350 degrees. Place the tofu in a large bowl and crumble. Add the parsley, salt, and pepper, and mix well. Taste to adjust seasoning. Spread a layer of the sauce in the bottom of a large baking dish. Top the sauce with a layer of noodles. Top the noodles with a layer of the tofu filling, repeat with another layer of noodles, and top with more sauce. Add a layer of textured soy protein. Repeat the process until all the components are used, ending with sauce. Sprinkle the shredded soy mozzarella on top of the final sauce layer. Bake for 45 minutes. Allow to set for 5 minutes before cutting.

*6 to 8 servings*

## Nutritional Analysis

| | | |
|---|---:|---|
| Kilocalories | 576 | Kc |
| Protein | 38.2 | Gm |
|   from soy | 25.7 | Gm |
| Fat | 16 | Gm |
| Percent of calories from fat | 24 | % |
| Cholesterol | 0 | mg |
| Dietary fiber | 6 | Gm |
| Sodium | 420 | mg |
| Calcium | 498 | mg |

# Tofu Lo Mein

*Linguine may be used quite successfully if the Asian pastas are unavailable.*

| | |
|---|---|
| 1 | 8-ounce package soba, udon, or lo mein noodles |
| 1 | teaspoon plus 1 tablespoon sesame oil |
| 1 | tablespoon safflower oil |
| 1/4 | cup minced scallions |
| 1 | teaspoon minced fresh ginger |
| 1/2 | cup sliced mushrooms |
| 1/2 | cup sliced carrots, blanched (see note page 82) |
| 2 | cups chopped bok choy |
| 8 | ounces extra-firm tofu, cut into 1/4-inch-thick strips |
| 1 | tablespoon low-sodium tamari |

Cook the noodles according to package directions. Drain, transfer to a bowl, and toss with 1 teaspoon sesame oil. Set aside. Heat the remaining sesame oil and safflower oil in a large skillet over medium-high heat, add the scallions and ginger, and stir-fry until fragrant, about 1 minute. Add the mushrooms, carrots, and bok choy, and continue stir-frying about 2 minutes. Add the tofu and tamari and continue to stir-fry 1 minute longer. Add the noodles and toss to combine.

*2 to 4 servings*

### Nutritional Analysis

| | | |
|---|---:|---|
| Kilocalories | 660 | Kc |
| Protein | 30.3 | Gm |
| from soy | 12.2 | Gm |
| Fat | 21 | Gm |
| Percent of calories from fat | 28 | % |
| Cholesterol | 0 | mg |
| Dietary fiber | 2 | Gm |
| Sodium | 1235 | mg |
| Calcium | 287 | mg |

# Pasta Primavera

*If miso paste is unavailable, substitute tamari or dry sherry for extra flavor. Sprinkle with soy parmesan, if desired.*

| | |
|---|---|
| 1 | tablespoon safflower oil |
| 1/2 | cup chopped red bell pepper |
| 1 | teaspoon minced garlic |
| 1/4 | cup minced scallions |
| 1/2 | cup sliced mushrooms |
| 1 | carrot, cut into 1/4-inch rounds, blanched (see note page 82) |
| 1 | cup broccoli florets, blanched |
| 2 | cups soy milk |
| 8 | ounces silken tofu |
| 1/2 | teaspoon salt |
| 1/4 | teaspoon freshly ground pepper |
| 1 | tablespoon cornstarch |
| 1 | tablespoon white miso paste |
| 1 | pound linguine, or other pasta |
| 1/4 | cup minced fresh parsley |

Heat the oil in a large skillet. Sauté the bell pepper, garlic, scallions, and mushrooms for 5 minutes. Add the carrots and broccoli and sauté 2 minutes longer. Set aside. In a food processor or blender, combine the soy milk, tofu, salt, pepper, and cornstarch. Place the tofu mixture in a small saucepan and heat, stirring constantly, to achieve a smooth sauce. In a small bowl, blend the miso paste with 1/4 cup of the sauce, and stir into the skillet. Taste to adjust seasonings. Keep the sauce warm. In the meantime, cook the pasta in a large pot of boiling salted water until tender but still firm, about 10 to 12 minutes. Drain well. Toss the pasta with the vegetables and sauce, sprinkle with parsley, and serve.

*4 to 6 servings*

### Nutritional Analysis

| | |
|---|---|
| Kilocalories | 562 Kc |
| Protein | 22.4 Gm |
| from soy | 6.5 Gm |
| Fat | 10 Gm |
| Percent of calories from fat | 15 % |
| Cholesterol | 0 mg |
| Dietary fiber | 6 Gm |
| Sodium | 488 mg |
| Calcium | 72 mg |

# CHATELAINE food express

# Quickies 2

**#4 IN THE SERIES!**

**V**egetarian cooking transforms from beige and dull to colorful and delicious – from mung beans and granola to mushroom risottos and Cajun pancakes – in this fourth addition to the *Chatelaine Food Express* series!

The A-Z listing of ingredients so popular in the bestselling *Quickies* returns here, and this time the focus is on vegetables, beans and grains. From

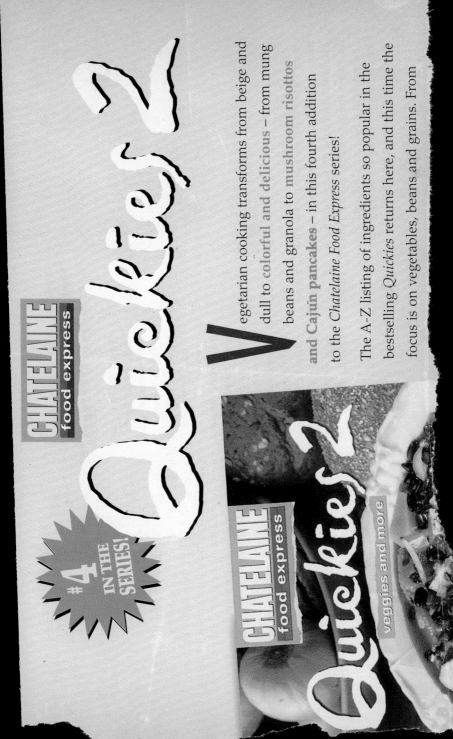

CHATELAINE food express

Quickies 2

veggies and more

This tasty colourful salad travels well.

## Fiesta bean salad

Here's a lower-fat version of a summer favourite filled with colourful peppers. Use whichever cans of beans you have on hand. There's enough protein from the beans that two cups (500 mL) of this salad will fill about one-quarter of your protein needs for the day.

**Preparation time** 30 minutes
**Makes** 10 cups (2.5 L), 10 servings

| | |
|---|---|
| 2 | (19-oz/540-mL) cans chickpeas or beans, such as mixed, kidney or Romano beans |
| 3 | sweet peppers, preferably 1 red, 1 green and 1 yellow |
| 4 | large plum tomatoes |
| 4 | green onions |
| 1/2 cup | (125 mL) chopped fresh coriander or parsley |
| 1/4 cup | (50 mL) red wine vinegar |
| 3 tsp | (15 mL) cumin |
| 2 tsp | (10 mL) chili powder |
| 1/2 tsp | (2 mL) salt |
| 2 | minced garlic cloves |
| 2 tbsp | (30 mL) olive oil |

**1.** Drain chickpeas or beans into a sieve or colander. Then rinse under cold running water and drain well. Place in a large mixing bowl. Seed and finely chop peppers and tomatoes. Thinly slice onions. Add to chickpeas along with coriander and gently mix.

**2.** In a small bowl, whisk vinegar with cumin, chili powder, salt and garlic. When thoroughly blended, slowly drizzle in oil while whisking constantly. Pour over chickpea mixture and gently mix to avoid breaking up chickpeas. Serve right away or cover and refrigerate up to 2 days. Flavours mingle as salad stands. Garnish with crisp tortilla chips and pieces of coriander.

**Nutrients per cup (250 mL)** 6.3 g protein, 4.4 g fat, 22.5 g carbohydrates, 1.7 mg iron, 36 mg calcium, 289 mg sodium, 3.7 g fibre, 147 calories • Excellent source of vitamin C • Good source of vitamin $B_6$ and folacin ▷

# Pasta with "Meaty" Tomato Sauce

*A healthy version of pasta with meat sauce. Sautéed ground tempeh or crumbled firm tofu can be used to replace the textured soy protein granules, if you prefer.*

  1   tablespoon olive oil
  1   cup minced onion
  1   teaspoon minced garlic
  1   6-ounce can tomato paste
  1   cup textured soy protein granules (TVP),
         combined with 1 cup water
  1   16-ounce can tomato puree
  1/4 cup minced fresh parsley
  1   teaspoon dried basil
  1/2 teaspoon dried oregano
  1/2 teaspoon salt
  1/8 teaspoon freshly ground pepper
  2   cups water
  1   pound linguine, or other pasta

Heat the oil in a large saucepan over medium heat, add the onion and garlic, cover, and cook for 5 minutes. Remove the lid and add the tomato paste to saucepan. Cook uncovered, stirring, 2 more minutes. Add the soy granules, tomato puree, parsley, basil, oregano, salt, and pepper to the saucepan with the 2 cups water. Simmer over medium-low heat for 1 hour, stirring occasionally. If the sauce becomes too thick, add more water.

Meanwhile, cook the pasta in a large pot of boiling salted water until tender but still firm, about 10 to 12 minutes.

Drain well. To serve, divide the hot pasta among individual serving plates and top with the sauce, or place the pasta in a shallow serving bowl and spoon the sauce over the top.

*6 servings*

### Nutritional Analysis

| | | |
|---|---:|---|
| Kilocalories | 417 | Kc |
| Protein | 23.2 | Gm |
| from soy | 10.8 | Gm |
| Fat | 4 | Gm |
| Percent of calories from fat | 8 | % |
| Cholesterol | 0 | mg |
| Dietary fiber | 8 | Gm |
| Sodium | 237 | mg |
| Calcium | 110 | mg |

# Spinach Tofu Casserole

1   tablespoon safflower oil
1   cup minced onion
1   10-ounce package frozen spinach,
      cooked and drained
1   pound firm tofu, drained
1   teaspoon salt
1/4 teaspoon pepper
      Pinch ground nutmeg
1/2 cup soy milk
3   cups cooked pasta shells, or other
      small, shaped pasta
1/2 cup shredded soy mozzarella

Preheat the oven to 350 degrees. Heat the oil in a large skillet over medium-high heat. Add the onion and cook for 5 minutes, or until soft. Squeeze the liquid from the spinach, chop, add to the onion, and set aside. In a food processor, combine the tofu, salt, pepper, and nutmeg. Add the soy milk. Process to blend. Combine the tofu mixture with the spinach mixture. Combine with the cooked pasta and adjust seasonings. Transfer the mixture to a lightly oiled casserole dish. Top with the soy cheese. Bake for 40 minutes, or until bubbly.

*4 to 6 servings*

### Nutritional Analysis

| | | |
|---|---:|---|
| Kilocalories | 329 | Kc |
| Protein | 21.4 | Gm |
| from soy | 15.7 | Gm |
| Fat | 12 | Gm |
| Percent of calories from fat | 33 | % |
| Cholesterol | 0 | mg |
| Dietary fiber | 3 | Gm |
| Sodium | 668 | mg |
| Calcium | 342 | mg |

# Ginger Tempeh Stir-Fry

*Serve this dish over rice.*

|         |                                               |
|--------:|-----------------------------------------------|
| 1       | pound tempeh                                  |
| 1½      | tablespoons cornstarch                        |
| 1½      | tablespoons water                             |
| 2       | tablespoons safflower oil                     |
| 1       | carrot, cut diagonally into ¼-inch slices     |
| 1       | teaspoon minced garlic                        |
| 2       | teaspoons minced fresh ginger                 |
| 2       | cups broccoli florets                         |
| 2       | tablespoons minced scallions                  |
| 2       | tablespoons dry sherry                        |
| 2       | tablespoons low-sodium tamari                 |
| ½       | cup water                                     |
| 1       | tablespoon cornstarch dissolved in            |
|         | 1½ tablespoons water                          |

Place the tempeh in a saucepan of boiling water. Reduce the heat to low and simmer for 10 minutes. Cool and cut into ½-inch cubes. Combine 1½ tablespoons cornstarch with 1½ tablespoons water in a shallow bowl. Add the tempeh, coating thoroughly. Refrigerate for 30 minutes. Heat the oil in a wok or skillet over high heat, and add the carrot. Stir in the garlic, ginger, and broccoli. Add the tempeh and stir-fry about 2 minutes. Add the scallions and stir-fry about 30 seconds. Stir in the sherry, tamari, ½ cup water, and cornstarch mixture and cook until the liquid thickens.

*4 servings*

## Nutritional Analysis

| | | |
|---|---:|---|
| Kilocalories | 360 | Kc |
| Protein | 25.6 | Gm |
| from soy | 22.4 | Gm |
| Fat | 16 | Gm |
| Percent of calories from fat | 37 | % |
| Cholesterol | 0 | mg |
| Dietary fiber | 12 | Gm |
| Sodium | 342 | mg |
| Calcium | 167 | mg |

# No-Meat Loaf

*Serve this delicious stand-in for meat loaf with Brown Sauce (recipe follows) and roasted potatoes. Dry-roasted soybeans are sold as a snack in natural food stores. They are sometimes called soy "nuts."*

| | |
|---|---|
| 1 | tablespoon safflower oil |
| 1/2 | cup minced onion |
| 1/4 | cup grated carrot |
| 1 | clove garlic, minced |
| 2 | cups grated tempeh |
| 1 | tablespoon minced fresh parsley |
| 2 | cups fresh bread crumbs |
| 1/2 | cup soft tofu |
| 1/2 | cup ground dry-roasted soybeans |
| 1 | cup cooked lentils |
| 1/8 | teaspoon cayenne |
| 1 | tablespoon low-sodium tamari |
| 1 | teaspoon salt, or less, to taste |
| 2 | tablespoons tahini |

Preheat oven to 350 degrees. Heat the oil in a large skillet. Sauté the onion and carrot over medium heat for 5 minutes. Add the garlic, tempeh, and parsley and sauté 2 minutes. Add the bread crumbs, tofu, and ground soybeans to the onion mixture in the skillet, stirring well. Mash the lentils with a fork or puree in a food processor, and add to the mixture. Stir, and continue sautéing over low heat. Season with cayenne, tamari, and salt to taste. Cook for 10 minutes. Remove from the heat and stir in the tahini. Pour the mixture

into an oiled 9 × 5 inch loaf pan. Bake the loaf about 45 minutes or until firm and golden brown. Let stand 5 minutes
before slicing.

*6 servings*

| Nutritional Analysis | | |
|---|---:|---|
| Kilocalories | 619 | Kc |
| Protein | 39.2 | Gm |
| from soy | 27.1 | Gm |
| Fat | 20 | Gm |
| Percent of calories from fat | 28 | % |
| Cholesterol | 0 | mg |
| Dietary fiber | 15 | Gm |
| Sodium | 1230 | mg |
| Calcium | 332 | mg |

# Brown Sauce

*A flavorful all-purpose brown sauce that can be used on anything from burgers and cutlets to grains and potatoes. You can add sautéed minced onions or sliced mushrooms for added flavor.*

1½   **cups water**
¼   **cup low-sodium tamari**
½   **teaspoon dried thyme**
⅛   **teaspoon freshly ground pepper**
2   **tablespoons cornstarch dissolved in**
2   **tablespoons water**
½   **cup soy milk**

Combine the 1½ cups water, tamari, thyme, and pepper in a small saucepan and bring to a boil over high heat. Reduce the heat to medium, whisk in the cornstarch mixture, and simmer, stirring, for 2 minutes, or until the sauce thickens. Slowly whisk in the soy milk, being careful not to boil. Adjust seasonings.

*Makes 2¼ cups*

### Nutritional Analysis

| | | |
|---|---:|---|
| Kilocalories | 9 | Kc |
| Protein | .6 | Gm |
|   from soy | .6 | Gm |
| Fat | 0 | Gm |
| Percent of calories from fat | 13 | % |
| Cholesterol | 0 | mg |
| Dietary fiber | 0 | Gm |
| Sodium | 136 | mg |
| Calcium | 3 | mg |

# Old-Fashioned Pot Pie

*For crust:*

    1   cup all-purpose flour
    1/2 teaspoon salt
    1/4 cup (1/2 stick) soy margarine
    2   tablespoons ice water

*For filling:*

    2   cups extra-firm tofu, cut into 1/4-inch dice
    1/2 cup cooked chopped onion
    3/4 cup diced cooked carrot
    3/4 cup frozen peas, thawed
    1/2 cup cooked diced potato
    1   tablespoon minced fresh parsley
    2   tablespoons safflower oil
    2   tablespoons all-purpose flour
    2   cups soy milk
    1/2 teaspoon salt
    1/4 teaspoon dried thyme
    1/8 teaspoon freshly ground pepper

To make the crust, combine the flour and 1/2 teaspoon salt in a food processor. Add the soy margarine, processing until the mixture resembles coarse crumbs. Slowly add the water, processing just until the dough forms a ball on top of the blade. Roll the dough on a lightly floured surface to 1/4-inch thickness, shaped to the size of a casserole dish. Set aside.

To make the filling, preheat the oven to 350 degrees. Place the tofu, onion, carrot, peas, potato, and parsley in a lightly oiled 1½-quart casserole dish. Heat the oil in a medium saucepan. Stir in the 2 tablespoons flour and cook, stirring constantly, for 2 minutes. Gradually add the soy milk to the saucepan, stirring until smooth. Bring the sauce to a boil, stirring. Remove the sauce from the heat. Add the salt, thyme, and pepper. Pour the sauce over the mixture in the casserole dish. Place the crust over the filled casserole, crimping the edges. Bake for 40 minutes or until the crust is lightly browned.

*6 servings*

| Nutritional Analysis | | |
|---|---|---|
| Kilocalories | 347 | Kc |
| Protein | 16.9 | Gm |
| from soy | 12.7 | Gm |
| Fat | 18 | Gm |
| Percent of calories from fat | 47 | % |
| Cholesterol | 0 | mg |
| Dietary fiber | 4 | Gm |
| Sodium | 509 | mg |
| Calcium | 66 | mg |

# Lorraine's New Quiche

*Quiche Lorraine gets a healthy makeover. Tofu replaces the eggs and cream, and tempeh bacon adds a hint of smoky flavor to this no-cholesterol version of an old favorite.*

*For crust:*

| | |
|---|---|
| 1 | cup all-purpose flour |
| 1/2 | teaspoon salt |
| 1/4 | cup (1/2 stick) soy margarine |
| 2 | tablespoons ice water |

*For filling:*

| | |
|---|---|
| 2 | tablespoons safflower oil |
| 1 | cup minced onion |
| 1/2 | cup chopped tempeh bacon |
| 1 | pound extra-firm silken tofu |
| 1/2 | teaspoon salt |
| 1/4 | teaspoon ground nutmeg |
| 1/8 | teaspoon cayenne |
| 1/2 | cup grated soy mozzarella |

To make the crust, combine the flour and salt in a food processor. Cut the margarine into small pieces and add to the flour. Pulse the mixture until crumbly. Add the water slowly, pulsing until the mixture forms a ball. Roll out on a floured board into a circle large enough to line a 9-inch pie pan. Place the dough in the pan, fitting against the sides and bottom, and crimp the edge of the dough with your fingers.

To make the filling, preheat the oven to 350 degrees. Heat the oil in a large skillet over medium heat. Add the onion, cover, and cook for 5 minutes, or until the onion softens.

Remove the cover, add the tempeh bacon, and continue cooking, stirring, until the bacon becomes crisp and browned. Set aside. Place the tofu in a food processor with the salt, nutmeg, and cayenne and blend until smooth and creamy. Combine the tofu mixture with the onion mixture, and fold in the soy cheese. Pour the filling mixture into the pie crust, and bake for 40 minutes or until the crust is browned and the filling is firm. Cool for several minutes before slicing.

*6 servings*

| Nutritional Analysis | | |
|---|---:|---|
| Kilocalories | 320 | Kc |
| Protein | 16.5 | Gm |
|    from soy | 14.1 | Gm |
| Fat | 20 | Gm |
| Percent of calories from fat | 54 | % |
| Cholesterol | 0 | mg |
| Dietary fiber | 2 | Gm |
| Sodium | 570 | mg |
| Calcium | 101 | mg |

# Barbecued Tofu

*This tasty sauce is also great with tempeh. Serve this dish over freshly cooked rice.*

      2    tablespoons safflower oil
    1/2    cup minced onion
      1    cup tomato sauce
      2    tablespoons brown sugar or honey
      2    tablespoons cider vinegar
      1    tablespoon prepared mustard
      1    tablespoon Worcestershire sauce
    1/8    teaspoon cayenne
    1/2    teaspoon salt
      1    pound firm tofu, cut into 1/2-inch slices

Heat 1 tablespoon of the oil in a large saucepan over medium-high heat, add the onion, cover, and cook 5 minutes or until the onion is soft. Add the remaining ingredients, except the tofu, to the saucepan. Bring to a boil, stirring. Reduce the heat and simmer for 20 minutes. Adjust seasonings. Meanwhile, heat the remaining oil in a skillet over medium-high heat. Add the tofu slices and cook until golden brown, turning once, about 2 minutes per side. When browned, add the sauce and simmer the tofu in the sauce for about 10 minutes, spooning the sauce over the tofu as it simmers.

*4 servings*

## Nutritional Analysis

| | | |
|---|---:|---|
| Kilocalories | 221 | Kc |
| Protein | 12.7 | Gm |
|   from soy | 11.3 | Gm |
| Fat | 12 | Gm |
| Percent of calories from fat | 47 | % |
| Cholesterol | 0 | mg |
| Dietary fiber | 1 | Gm |
| Sodium | 615 | mg |
| Calcium | 217 | mg |

# Tempeh Cutlets with Creamy Mustard Sauce

1    pound tempeh, cut into 4 equal cutlets
2    tablespoons safflower oil
1/4  cup minced onion
2    tablespoons minced scallions
1/2  teaspoon minced garlic
1/4  cup water
3    tablespoons Dijon mustard
1/2  cup silken tofu, drained and patted dry
1/4  cup soy milk
1    tablespoon fresh lemon juice
1    tablespoon minced fresh parsley
1/4  teaspoon salt
1/8  teaspoon freshly ground pepper

Place the tempeh in a saucepan of boiling water. Reduce the heat to low and simmer 10 minutes. Remove the tempeh from the water and pat dry. Heat 1 tablespoon of the oil in a large skillet over medium-high heat. Add the tempeh and cook on both sides until golden, about 2 minutes per side. Keep the tempeh warm in the oven.

Add the remaining oil to the skillet over medium heat, add the onion, and cook 5 minutes, or until soft. Add the scallions and garlic and stir 1 minute. Increase the heat to high, add 1/4 cup water, and cook until reduced by half, about 2 minutes. Reduce the heat to low, add the mustard, tofu, and soy milk, and cook, stirring, until the sauce is thick. Blend in the lemon juice. Add the parsley, salt, and pepper. To serve, place the cutlets on plates and spoon the sauce over them.

*4 servings*

## Nutritional Analysis

| | | |
|---|---|---|
| Kilocalories | 330 | Kc |
| Protein | 24.5 | Gm |
|   from soy | 23.4 | Gm |
| Fat | 18 | Gm |
| Percent of calories from fat | 45 | % |
| Cholesterol | 0 | mg |
| Dietary fiber | 9 | Gm |
| Sodium | 222 | mg |
| Calcium | 139 | mg |

# Sweet-and-Sour Tempeh

*This healthful interpretation of a Chinese restaurant favorite can also be made with firm tofu.*

| | |
|---|---|
| 1 | pound tempeh |
| 1/4 | cup pineapple juice (from canned pineapple, below) |
| 3 | tablespoons fresh lemon juice |
| 2 | tablespoons ketchup |
| 2 | tablespoons low-sodium tamari |
| 1 | tablespoon sugar (or a natural sweetener) |
| 1 | tablespoon cornstarch |
| 1 | tablespoon safflower oil |
| 1 | green or red bell pepper, chopped |
| 1 | tablespoon minced scallion |
| 1 | teaspoon minced fresh ginger |
| 1 | teaspoon minced garlic |
| 3/4 | cup canned pineapple chunks |
| | Freshly cooked rice |

Place the tempeh in a saucepan of boiling water. Reduce the heat to low and simmer for 10 minutes. Drain, pat dry, and cut into 1-inch cubes. Set aside. Combine the pineapple juice, lemon juice, ketchup, tamari, sugar, and cornstarch in small bowl; stir well to combine. Heat the oil in a skillet over medium-high heat. Add the bell pepper, tempeh, scallion, ginger, and garlic, and cook for about 5 minutes, or until the bell pepper begins to soften and the tempeh is golden brown. Reduce the heat to medium, add the sauce mixture and pineapple. Cook, stirring, until the ingredients are well combined and the sauce has thickened, about 2 minutes. Serve over rice.

*4 servings*

## Nutritional Analysis

| | | |
|---|---:|---|
| Kilocalories | 332 | Kc |
| Protein | 23.3 | Gm |
| from soy | 22.4 | Gm |
| Fat | 12 | Gm |
| Percent of calories from fat | 31 | % |
| Cholesterol | 0 | mg |
| Dietary fiber | 10 | Gm |
| Sodium | 381 | mg |
| Calcium | 128 | mg |

# Tempeh Teriyaki

1    pound tempeh, cut into 1/4-inch-thick slices
1/4  cup fresh lemon juice
1/4  cup low-sodium tamari
1    teaspoon minced garlic
1    tablespoon honey (or other sweetener)
2    tablespoons toasted sesame oil
1    tablespoon safflower oil

Place the tempeh in a saucepan of boiling water. Reduce the heat to low and simmer for 10 minutes. Drain and place in a large, shallow dish. In a small bowl combine the lemon juice, tamari, garlic, and honey. Slowly add the sesame oil in a stream, whisking until it is well blended. Pour the marinade over the tempeh, turning the tempeh to coat, and refrigerate the tempeh in the marinade for several hours or overnight, turning once. Remove the tempeh from the marinade. Heat the safflower oil in a large skillet and sauté the tempeh until golden brown on both sides, about 2 minutes per side. Add the reserved marinade and simmer for 10 minutes, turning the tempeh once.

*4 servings*

## Nutritional Analysis

| | | |
|---|---:|---|
| Kilocalories | 335 | Kc |
| Protein | 23.2 | Gm |
| from soy | 23.1 | Gm |
| Fat | 17 | Gm |
| Percent of calories from fat | 44 | % |
| Cholesterol | 0 | mg |
| Dietary fiber | 8 | Gm |
| Sodium | 541 | mg |
| Calcium | 113 | mg |

# Tofu Stroganoff

| | |
|---|---|
| 1 | pound firm tofu, cut into 1-inch cubes |
| 1/4 | teaspoon paprika |
| 1/2 | teaspoon salt |
| 1/8 | teaspoon freshly ground pepper |
| 2 | tablespoons safflower oil |
| 1/4 | cup dry sherry or brandy |
| 1/2 | cup chopped onion |
| 1 | cup sliced mushrooms |
| 1 | tablespoon tomato paste |
| 3 | tablespoons low-sodium tamari |
| 1 | teaspoon prepared mustard |
| 1/2 | teaspoon minced fresh thyme or 1/4 teaspoon dried |
| 2 | tablespoons cornstarch dissolved in 2 tablespoons water |
| 1 | cup soy milk |
| | Freshly cooked noodles |
| | Tofu Sour Cream (recipe follows) |
| 1 | tablespoon minced fresh parsley |

Season the tofu with paprika, salt, and pepper. Heat 1 tablespoon of the oil in a large skillet over medium-high heat and add the tofu to the skillet, stirring to brown on all sides. Carefully add the sherry or brandy, and shake the pan until the flame subsides. Transfer the tofu to a platter and keep warm in the oven.

Add the remaining tablespoon of oil to the skillet, add the onion, cover, and cook over medium heat until softened, about 5 minutes. Remove the lid, add the mushrooms, and cook 2 minutes longer, stirring occasionally. Add the tomato paste, tamari, mustard, thyme, and salt and pepper to taste. Stir in the cornstarch mixture. Reduce the heat to low and slowly add the soy milk, stirring until the sauce thickens, about 2 minutes. Add the reserved tofu. Cook gently for 3 to 5 minutes on low heat. Adjust seasonings. Serve over cooked noodles, topped with Tofu Sour Cream, and sprinkle with parsley.

*4 servings*

### Nutritional Analysis

| | | |
|---|---:|---|
| Kilocalories | 246 | Kc |
| Protein | 15.3 | Gm |
| from soy | 14.3 | Gm |
| Fat | 13 | Gm |
| Percent of calories from fat | 47 | % |
| Cholesterol | 0 | mg |
| Dietary fiber | 2 | Gm |
| Sodium | 788 | mg |
| Calcium | 210 | mg |

# Tofu Sour Cream

1   cup firm silken tofu, patted dry
2   tablespoons fresh lemon juice
1   tablespoon safflower oil
1/4  teaspoon prepared mustard
1/2  teaspoon salt

Combine all of the ingredients in a blender or food processor and process until smooth. Chill before serving.

*Makes about 1 1/2 cups*

| Nutritional Analysis | |
| --- | ---: |
| Kilocalories | 22 Kc |
| Protein | 1.0 Gm |
| from soy | 1.0 Gm |
| Fat | 2 Gm |
| Percent of calories from fat | 69 % |
| Cholesterol | 0 mg |
| Dietary fiber | 0 Gm |
| Sodium | 100 mg |
| Calcium | 7 mg |

# Jambalaya

*This flavorful new take on jambalaya uses a variety of foods high in soy protein. Filé powder is a Creole spice mixture made from sassafras leaves and is available in most supermarkets.*

2   tablespoons safflower oil
1   cup chopped onion
1/2 cup chopped celery
1   teaspoon minced garlic
1   green bell pepper, chopped
1   28-ounce can peeled tomatoes, chopped
2   tablespoons tomato paste
1   teaspoon filé powder
1   teaspoon salt
1   tablespoon chopped fresh parsley
1   teaspoon Tabasco sauce
4   ounces tempeh
4   ounces extra-firm tofu, cut into 1/2-inch cubes
8   ounces soy sausage links, cut into 1-inch pieces
    Freshly cooked rice

In a large pot, heat 1 tablespoon of the oil over medium heat, and add the onion, celery, garlic, and bell pepper. Sauté 5 minutes, or until the vegetables begin to soften. Add the tomatoes, tomato paste, filé powder, salt, parsley, and Tabasco sauce. Cover and simmer 20 minutes, or until the vegetables are soft. If the sauce becomes too thick, add 1/2 cup water. Meanwhile, poach the tempeh in a small saucepan of boiling water. Reduce the heat to low and simmer for 10 minutes. Drain and cut the tempeh into 1/2-inch cubes.

Heat the remaining 1 tablespoon oil in a skillet over medium-high heat. Add the tofu, meatless sausage, and tempeh and brown lightly. Stir the soy "meats" into the sauce. Cook 5 minutes longer. Adjust seasonings. Serve over freshly cooked rice.

*6 servings*

| Nutritional Analysis | | |
|---|---:|---|
| Kilocalories | 245 | Kc |
| Protein | 14.7 | Gm |
| from soy | 12.5 | Gm |
| Fat | 14 | Gm |
| Percent of calories from fat | 48 | % |
| Cholesterol | 0 | mg |
| Dietary fiber | 5 | Gm |
| Sodium | 959 | mg |
| Calcium | 123 | mg |

# Fiesta Bake

*Assemble this quick and easy casserole ahead of time for a zesty no-fuss dinner.*

1    tablespoon safflower oil
1/2   cup minced scallions
2    cups rehydrated textured soy protein granules (TVP)
1    teaspoon chili powder
2    cups prepared salsa
2    cups firm silken tofu, drained
1    4-ounce can diced green chilies
2    tablespoons fresh lime juice
1/2   teaspoon salt
1/8   teaspoon freshly ground pepper
1    cup crumbled corn chips
1/2   cup grated soy cheddar cheese

Heat the oil in a medium skillet over medium heat. Add the scallions and cook 2 minutes. Add the soy granules and chili powder, cook for 1 minute, and set aside. Lightly oil a 2-quart baking dish or coat it with nonstick cooking spray. Spread half of the salsa on the bottom of the dish, cover the salsa layer with the soy protein mixture, and set aside. In a small bowl, combine the tofu with the chilies, lime juice, salt, and pepper, whisking until smooth. Pour the tofu mixture over the top layer of the casserole. Top the tofu layer with the remaining salsa. The casserole can be made ahead to this point and refrigerated until ready to use. To bake, bring it to room temperature, cover, and bake in a 350-degree oven for 20 minutes. Remove the cover, top with the corn chips and soy cheese, and bake, uncovered, about 10 minutes longer.

*8 servings*

## Nutritional Analysis

| | | |
|---|---|---|
| Kilocalories | 193 | Kc |
| Protein | 11.3 | Gm |
| from soy | 9.7 | Gm |
| Fat | 11 | Gm |
| Percent of calories from fat | 50 | % |
| Cholesterol | 0 | mg |
| Dietary fiber | 3 | Gm |
| Sodium | 274 | mg |
| Calcium | 179 | mg |

# Great Goulash

*What a combination: old-world flavor and protein-rich soy foods, served over freshly cooked noodles.*

1 pound tempeh
2 tablespoons safflower oil
1 cup chopped onion
1/2 cup sliced carrot
1/4 cup chopped celery
2 tablespoons sweet Hungarian paprika
2 tablespoons all-purpose flour
1 tablespoon tomato paste
1 cup sauerkraut, rinsed and drained
1/4 cup dry white wine
1 cup water
   Salt and freshly ground pepper to taste
1 cup silken tofu, drained and pressed
1 tablespoon fresh lemon juice
   Freshly cooked noodles

Place the tempeh in a saucepan of boiling water. Reduce the heat to low and simmer for 10 minutes. Drain and cut into 1-inch cubes. Heat 1 tablespoon of the oil in a large skillet over medium heat. Add the tempeh and cook until golden brown on all sides, about 5 minutes. Remove from the skillet and keep warm. In the same skillet, add the remaining oil, onion, carrot, and celery. Cover and cook over medium heat for 5 minutes, or until the vegetables begin to soften. Stir in the paprika and cook 2 minutes. Add the flour and cook, stirring, 2 minutes longer. Stir in the tomato paste until smooth. Add the sauerkraut, wine, and 1 cup water. Stir over low heat until it comes to a boil. Season with salt and pepper to taste. Reduce the heat to very low and simmer 5 minutes. In a small bowl, combine the tofu and lemon juice until well blended. Slowly whisk the tofu mixture into the goulash a little at a time, blending with each addition. Add the reserved tempeh and cook gently to heat through, about 10 minutes. Serve over noodles.

*4 servings*

### Nutritional Analysis

| | | |
|---|---:|---|
| Kilocalories | 390 | Kc |
| Protein | 26.7 | Gm |
| from soy | 24.5 | Gm |
| Fat | 18 | Gm |
| Percent of calories from fat | 39 | % |
| Cholesterol | 0 | mg |
| Dietary fiber | 12 | Gm |
| Sodium | 418 | mg |
| Calcium | 166 | mg |

# Simmered Soy Stew

2　tablespoons olive oil
1　large onion, cut into $1/4$-inch-thick wedges
2　carrots, cut into $1/4$-inch slices
1　teaspoon minced garlic
1　baking potato, peeled and cut into
　　$1/4$-inch-thick slices
1　red or green bell pepper, cut into 1-inch dice
1　28-ounce can peeled tomatoes, chopped
1　tablespoon minced fresh parsley
1　teaspoon minced fresh basil, or
　　$1/4$ teaspoon dried
1　tablespoon low-sodium tamari
1　cup water
　　Salt and freshly ground pepper to taste
8　ounces tempeh, cut into $1/2$-inch cubes
8　ounces extra-firm tofu, cut into $1/2$-inch cubes

Heat 1 tablespoon of the oil in a large saucepan over medium heat. Add the onion and carrots, cover, and cook until the vegetables begin to soften, about 5 minutes. Reduce the heat to low. Add the garlic, potato, bell pepper, tomatoes, parsley, basil, tamari, and 1 cup water. Season with salt and pepper to taste. Cover and cook until the vegetables are tender, about 30 minutes, adding more water if necessary. While the vegetables are cooking, place the tempeh in a saucepan of boiling water. Reduce the heat to low and simmer for 10 minutes. Drain and pat dry. Heat the remaining oil in a skillet over medium heat, sauté the tempeh and tofu until golden, and season with salt and pepper. Add the tempeh and tofu to the stew and simmer 5 minutes longer.

*6 servings*

| Nutritional Analysis | | |
|---|---:|---|
| Kilocalories | 249 | Kc |
| Protein | 14.3 | Gm |
| from soy | 11.2 | Gm |
| Fat | 9 | Gm |
| Percent of calories from fat | 32 | % |
| Cholesterol | 0 | mg |
| Dietary fiber | 7 | Gm |
| Sodium | 336 | mg |
| Calcium | 153 | mg |

# Curried Tofu

*This exotically spiced dish is simply wonderful served over freshly cooked rice with your favorite chutney.*

| | |
|---|---|
| 1 | tablespoon safflower oil |
| 1 | cup chopped onion |
| 1/2 | cup diced fresh or canned jalapeño chilies |
| 1 | teaspoon minced garlic |
| 1 | teaspoon minced fresh ginger |
| 1 | tablespoon curry powder |
| 1/2 | cup water |
| 1 | pound extra-firm tofu, cut into 1/2-inch pieces |
| 1 1/2 | cups soy milk |
| 1/2 | cup raisins |
| 1 | teaspoon sugar (or a natural sweetener) |
| | Salt and freshly ground black pepper |

Heat the oil in a large saucepan over medium heat. Add the onion, cover, and cook until softened, about 5 minutes. Add the chilies, garlic, and ginger and cook about 2 minutes longer. Stir in the curry powder and cook 2 to 3 minutes, stirring occasionally. Add about 1/2 cup water and simmer 15 minutes, or until the vegetables are soft. Add the tofu, soy milk, raisins, sugar, and salt and pepper to taste. Simmer about 10 minutes longer to allow the flavors to intensify.

*4 servings*

## Nutritional Analysis

| | | |
|---|---|---|
| Kilocalories | 245 | Kc |
| Protein | 15.3 | Gm |
| from soy | 13.8 | Gm |
| Fat | 10 | Gm |
| Percent of calories from fat | 36 | % |
| Cholesterol | 0 | mg |
| Dietary fiber | 3 | Gm |
| Sodium | 277 | mg |
| Calcium | 223 | mg |

# Tofu Noodle Casserole

1   tablespoon safflower oil
1   pound extra-firm tofu, cut into 1/2-inch cubes
1   cup sliced mushrooms
1   tablespoon minced scallion
1/4 teaspoon salt
1/8 teaspoon freshly ground pepper
2   tablespoons dry sherry
1   cup water
1   vegetable bouillon cube
2   tablespoons cornstarch dissolved in
      2 tablespoons water
1   cup soy milk
4   cups cooked linguine, or other pasta
1   cup grated soy mozzarella

Preheat the oven to 375 degrees. Heat the oil in a large skillet over medium-high heat. Add the tofu, mushrooms, scallion, salt, and pepper, and cook 2 minutes, stirring occasionally. Add the sherry and remove from the heat. In a medium saucepan, heat the water and bouillon cube to boiling, stirring to dissolve the bouillon cube. Whisk in the cornstarch mixture, and continue stirring to thicken. Reduce the heat to low and slowly stir in the soy milk. Combine the cooked pasta with the tofu mixture, add the sauce, and mix well. Transfer the mixture to a lightly oiled baking dish, and top with grated soy cheese. Bake 30 minutes.

*6 servings*

## Nutritional Analysis

| | | |
|---|---|---|
| Kilocalories | 311 | Kc |
| Protein | 18.1 | Gm |
| from soy | 13.3 | Gm |
| Fat | 11 | Gm |
| Percent of calories from fat | 31 | % |
| Cholesterol | 0 | mg |
| Dietary fiber | 3 | Gm |
| Sodium | 317 | mg |
| Calcium | 224 | mg |

# Tofu Cutlets with Creamy Mushroom Sauce

*The onion imparts a rich flavor to the creamy sauce, which can be used to liven up a variety of recipes, including grains, pastas, and vegetable dishes.*

    2    cups soy milk
    3    tablespoons safflower oil
    1/3  cup chopped onion
    2    tablespoons all-purpose flour
    1    cup sliced mushrooms
    1/2  teaspoon salt
    1/4  teaspoon freshly ground pepper
         Pinch dried thyme
    1    pound extra-firm tofu, cut into 1/2-inch slices
    2    tablespoons minced fresh parsley

Heat the soy milk in a small saucepan, being careful not to boil. Keep warm. Heat 2 tablespoons of the oil in a medium saucepan over medium heat. Add the onion, cover, and cook 5 minutes or until softened. Remove the lid, reduce the heat to low, add the flour, and cook for 2 minutes, stirring constantly. Slowly add the soy milk, whisking constantly. Add the mushrooms, salt, pepper, and thyme. Continue to cook for 2 to 3 minutes, stirring frequently. Keep warm. Meanwhile, heat the remaining oil in a large skillet over medium-high heat. Add the tofu, season with salt and pepper, and cook until golden brown, about 2 minutes per side. Transfer to a plate, spoon the sauce over the cutlets, and sprinkle with parsley.

*4 servings*

## Nutritional Analysis

| | | |
|---|---:|---|
| Kilocalories | 254 | Kc |
| Protein | 15.6 | Gm |
|    from soy | 14.1 | Gm |
| Fat | 17 | Gm |
| Percent of calories from fat | 60 | % |
| Cholesterol | 0 | mg |
| Dietary fiber | 2 | Gm |
| Sodium | 320 | mg |
| Calcium | 201 | mg |

# Spinach-Stuffed Pasta Shells
# with Cream Sauce

16 to 20  large pasta shells, cooked al dente
    1  10-ounce package frozen chopped spinach, thawed
    2  cups firm tofu, drained and crumbled
  1/4  cup minced scallions
      Salt and freshly ground pepper to taste
    2  tablespoons safflower oil
    2  tablespoons all-purpose flour
    2  cups hot soy milk
  1/8  teaspoon ground nutmeg
    1  cup bread crumbs
  1/2  cup shredded soy mozzarella
    2  tablespoons soy margarine, melted

Preheat the oven to 350 degrees. Drain the cooked pasta shells in a colander and run under cold water to stop the cooking process. Reserve. Squeeze the spinach in a towel to remove liquid. Place in a bowl, add the tofu, scallions, and salt and pepper to taste. Mix well and set aside.

Heat the oil in a medium saucepan over medium heat, stir in the flour, and cook 2 minutes. Reduce the heat to low. Whisk in the hot soy milk and cook for 2 minutes, stirring constantly to thicken. Add the nutmeg and salt and pepper to taste. Remove the sauce from the heat.

Coat a large shallow baking dish with vegetable cooking spray, and spread a layer of sauce on the bottom of the dish. Fill the shells with the spinach stuffing, using a small spoon and being careful not to overstuff. Place the stuffed shells in the dish in a single layer. Spoon the remaining sauce over the shells. In a small bowl, with a fork, combine the bread crumbs, soy cheese, and margarine. Sprinkle over the casserole. Cover and bake for 20 minutes. Uncover, and bake an additional 10 minutes to lightly brown the topping.

*4 servings*

### Nutritional Analysis

| | | |
|---|---:|---|
| Kilocalories | 556 | Kc |
| Protein | 28.4 | Gm |
| from soy | 18.2 | Gm |
| Fat | 24 | Gm |
| Percent of calories from fat | 39 | % |
| Cholesterol | 0 | mg |
| Dietary fiber | 6 | Gm |
| Sodium | 415 | mg |
| Calcium | 435 | mg |

# Macaroni and Soy Cheese

*Everyone's favorite comfort food, using protein-rich soy foods instead of dairy.*

|       |                                          |
|-------|------------------------------------------|
| 2     | tablespoons safflower oil                |
| 1     | small onion, minced                      |
| 2     | tablespoons all-purpose flour            |
| 2     | cups hot soy milk                        |
| 1/2   | teaspoon salt                            |
| 1/8   | teaspoon cayenne                         |
| 1     | pound elbow macaroni, cooked and drained |
| 1 1/2 | cups grated soy cheddar cheese           |
| 1     | cup bread crumbs                         |
| 2     | tablespoons melted soy margarine         |
| 1/2   | teaspoon paprika                         |

Preheat the oven to 350 degrees. Heat the oil in a saucepan over medium heat, add the onion, cover, and cook 5 minutes, or until soft. Remove the lid, stir in the flour, and cook for 2 minutes. Reduce the heat to low and slowly whisk in the soy milk. Continue to cook, stirring, for 2 minutes, or until the mixture thickens. Season with salt and cayenne. Combine the sauce with the cooked pasta and the soy cheddar. Spoon into a 9 × 13-inch baking dish. In a small bowl, combine the bread crumbs, margarine, and paprika, and sprinkle over the top of the casserole. Bake for 30 minutes, or until hot and bubbly.

*4 to 6 servings*

## Nutritional Analysis

| | | |
|---|---|---|
| Kilocalories | 830 | Kc |
| Protein | 32.5 | Gm |
| from soy | 13.8 | Gm |
| Fat | 27 | Gm |
| Percent of calories from fat | 29 | % |
| Cholesterol | 0 | mg |
| Dietary fiber | 8 | Gm |
| Sodium | 694 | mg |
| Calcium | 291 | mg |

# CHAPTER SEVEN

# Desserts

D o you think that you'll have to give up delights such as ice cream and cheesecake because of their high cholesterol content? Think again. When made with tofu and soy milk, not only can you eat these delicious temptations, you are actually *encouraged* to eat them in moderation as part of a plan to lower your cholesterol.

Peaches and "Cream" Pie, Almost-Instant Chocolate Mousse, and Blueberry Cheesecake may sound sinfully indulgent, but when made with tofu, they can actually be good for you. As with all desserts—and all food, for that matter—you are encouraged to use common sense, but it will be hard not to "eat the whole thing" when you try the Peanut Butter Pie. Though not "diet foods," and certainly not low in calories, these desserts are just like the real things—except for two important factors: They each contain several grams of soy protein, and they contain no cholesterol.

# Fresh Fruit with Creamy Lemon Sauce

*The lemon juice in the creamy sauce brings out the natural sweetness of the fruit. This dessert is especially satisfying after a heavy meal when you want something light yet delicious.*

| | |
|---|---|
| 1 | cup firm silken tofu, drained and pressed |
| 1/2 | cup honey (or other natural sweetener) |
| 1/4 | cup fresh lemon juice |
| 1 | teaspoon grated lemon zest |
| 1/2 | teaspoon ground ginger (optional) |
| 1/8 | teaspoon paprika |
| | Pinch turmeric |
| 4 | cups assorted seasonal fruit (cantaloupe, plums, strawberries, grapes, etc.) |
| | Fresh mint leaves (garnish) |

In a bowl or food processor combine the tofu, honey, lemon juice, lemon zest, ginger, paprika, and turmeric. Mix until well blended, and chill until serving time. Meanwhile, prepare the fruit by cutting it into bite-sized pieces and placing in a bowl. To serve, spoon the fruit into individual dessert dishes and top with a spoonful of sauce. Garnish with mint leaves and serve.

*4 servings*

## Nutritional Analysis

| | | |
|---|---:|---|
| Kilocalories | 245 | Kc |
| Protein | 5.6 | Gm |
|   from soy | 4.1 | Gm |
| Fat | 2 | Gm |
| Percent of calories from fat | 8 | % |
| Cholesterol | 0 | mg |
| Dietary fiber | 2 | Gm |
| Sodium | 27 | mg |
| Calcium | 38 | mg |

# Almost-Instant Chocolate Mousse

*This easy-to-prepare indulgence is made with tofu chocolate bars, which are available at natural-food stores. Regular chocolate chips may be substituted, if desired.*

2   8-ounce tofu chocolate candy bars
1   teaspoon vanilla extract
4   cups Tofu Whipped Cream (recipe follows)
    Grated tofu chocolate or chopped almonds (garnish)

Melt the tofu chocolate bars in the top of a double boiler set over hot, but not boiling, water. Stir in the vanilla extract. Remove the top of the boiler from the hot water and allow to cool to room temperature. Fold the chocolate mixture into the Tofu Whipped Cream. Divide the mousse evenly among dessert dishes. Refrigerate several hours until well chilled. Garnish with grated tofu chocolate or chopped almonds and serve.

*8 servings*

### Nutritional Analysis

| | | |
|---|---:|---|
| Kilocalories | 581 | Kc |
| Protein | 8.2 | Gm |
|   from soy | 7.0 | Gm |
| Fat | 7 | Gm |
| Percent of calories from fat | 15 | % |
| Cholesterol | 0 | mg |
| Dietary fiber | 0 | Gm |
| Sodium | 27 | mg |
| Calcium | 108 | mg |

# Tofu Whipped Cream

*An easy-to-prepare, no-cholesterol stand-in for a favorite topping.*

1   cup silken tofu, drained and patted dry
1/2   cup honey (or other natural sweetener)
1   tablespoon safflower oil
1   teaspoon vanilla extract
    Pinch salt

Place all the ingredients in a blender and blend until smooth and well combined. Chill before using.

*Makes 1 1/2 cups*

| Nutritional Analysis | |
|---|---|
| Kilocalories | 65 Kc |
| Protein | 1.0 Gm |
|   from soy | 1.0 Gm |
| Fat | 2 Gm |
| Percent of calories from fat | 23 % |
| Cholesterol | 0 mg |
| Dietary fiber | 0 Gm |
| Sodium | 2 mg |
| Calcium | 7 mg |

# Fresh Strawberry Pudding

*Use the ripest strawberries you can find for this cool and creamy dessert.*

2    pints strawberries, hulled
1    cup firm silken tofu, drained and patted dry
2    tablespoons sugar (or a natural sweetener)
1    tablespoon safflower oil
1/2  teaspoon fresh lemon juice
     Pinch salt
     Fresh mint leaves (garnish)

Place the hulled strawberries in a food processor and puree. Add the remaining ingredients (except mint leaves) and process until thoroughly mixed. Transfer to dessert dishes and serve chilled, garnished with fresh mint leaves.

*6 servings*

| Nutritional Analysis | | |
|---|---:|---|
| Kilocalories | 89 | Kc |
| Protein | 3.3 | Gm |
| from soy | 2.7 | Gm |
| Fat | 4 | Gm |
| Percent of calories from fat | 35 | % |
| Cholesterol | 0 | mg |
| Dietary fiber | 2 | Gm |
| Sodium | 15 | mg |
| Calcium | 26 | mg |

# Pineapple-Almond Bread Pudding

1   cup soft silken tofu, drained
1   quart vanilla soy milk, or more to taste
1   loaf bread, cubed (about 8 cups)
3/4  cup brown sugar (or a natural sweetener)
1   teaspoon ground ginger
3   cups chopped pineapple, fresh or canned
1   cup chopped almonds
1/2  cup flaked coconut

In a small bowl, combine the tofu with 1/2 cup soy milk until well blended. Reserve. Place the bread cubes in a large bowl and pour the remaining soy milk and sugar over them, tossing to coat. Let the bread stand for 1 hour to soak up liquid. Add more soy milk as needed to soften the bread cubes. Preheat the oven to 350 degrees. Lightly oil a 9 × 13-inch baking dish and set aside. Mix the reserved tofu mixture into the soaked bread, along with the ginger, pineapple, almonds, and coconut. Pour the mixture into the prepared baking dish and bake for 45 minutes or until firm.

*8 servings*

## Nutritional Analysis

| | | |
|---|---:|---|
| Kilocalories | 428 | Kc |
| Protein | 14.5 | Gm |
| from soy | 4.8 | Gm |
| Fat | 16 | Gm |
| Percent of calories from fat | 32 | % |
| Cholesterol | 0 | mg |
| Dietary fiber | 11 | Gm |
| Sodium | 402 | mg |
| Calcium | 120 | mg |

# Van-Choc-Straw "Ice Cream" Cake

*No time to bake doesn't have to mean no dessert. This special cake can be assembled in a flash. Tofu ice cream is available in natural-food stores.*

1   package (about 2 cups) fat-free chocolate cookies
2   tablespoons melted soy margarine
1   quart vanilla tofu "ice cream," softened
1   jar fruit-sweetened strawberry jam
1   cup sliced fresh strawberries

Place the cookies in a food processor and pulse to make crumbs. Add the melted margarine and combine. Coat the bottom and sides of a 9-inch springform pan with vegetable cooking spray and press the crumb mixture onto the bottom and sides of the pan. Place in the freezer to set. Press the softened tofu "ice cream" into the crust, smoothing the top with a spatula. Place in the freezer for several hours to firm up. When ready to serve, place the jam in a food processor to achieve spreadable consistency. Remove the sides from the springform pan. Spread the fruit topping over the top of the cake. Arrange the fresh strawberry slices on top of the cake, along the outside edge.

*8 servings*

## Nutritional Analysis

| | | |
|---|---:|---|
| Kilocalories | 350 | Kc |
| Protein | 3.2 | Gm |
| from soy | 2.0 | Gm |
| Fat | 14 | Gm |
| Percent of calories from fat | 35 | % |
| Cholesterol | 0 | mg |
| Dietary fiber | 2 | Gm |
| Sodium | 369 | mg |
| Calcium | 11 | mg |

# Peaches and "Cream" Pie

    1   cup all-purpose flour
   1/4  teaspoon salt
   1/4  cup (1/2 stick) soy margarine, cut into pieces
    2   tablespoons water
  11/2  cups firm silken tofu, drained and patted dry
   1/2  cup sugar (or a natural sweetener)
    1   tablespoon safflower oil
    1   teaspoon vanilla extract
  21/2  cups peeled peach slices
   1/2  cup fruit-sweetened peach preserves
   1/2  teaspoon fresh lemon juice
   1/8  teaspoon ground ginger

Preheat the oven to 350 degrees. Place the flour and salt in a food processor and combine. Add the margarine and process until crumbly. With the machine running, slowly add the 2 tablespoons water to form a dough ball. On a lightly floured surface, roll out the dough, and arrange in a 9-inch pie plate, trimming the dough and fluting the edge. Prick holes in the bottom of the crust with a fork. Place the pie crust in the oven and bake for 10 minutes. Remove from the oven and set aside.

In a food processor, combine the tofu, sugar, oil, and vanilla, and blend thoroughly. Pour into the prepared crust, and bake for 30 minutes. Remove from the oven and allow to cool. Beginning at the outer edge, arrange peach slices on top of the pie in a circular pattern until the entire surface is covered. Puree the preserves in a blender or food processor with the lemon juice and ginger to achieve a smooth consistency. Spoon the peach glaze over the pie. Refrigerate at least 1 hour to set the glaze before serving.

*8 servings*

## Nutritional Analysis

| | | |
|---|---:|---|
| Kilocalories | 238 | Kc |
| Protein | 5.3 | Gm |
| from soy | 3.5 | Gm |
| Fat | 9 | Gm |
| Percent of calories from fat | 32 | % |
| Cholesterol | 0 | mg |
| Dietary fiber | 1 | Gm |
| Sodium | 175 | mg |
| Calcium | 25 | mg |

# Peanut Butter Pie

*Just a small wedge of this rich dessert is enough to satisfy any sweet tooth.*

- 2 cups fat-free chocolate cookie crumbs
- 1/2 cup ground dry-roasted soybeans
- 1/4 cup (1/2 stick) soy margarine, melted
- 1/2 gallon vanilla tofu "ice cream," softened
- 2 cups creamy peanut butter
- 1/2 cup honey (or other natural sweetener)
  tofu chocolate curls or shavings (garnish)

Preheat the oven to 350 degrees. Coat a 9-inch springform pan with nonstick cooking spray. In a medium bowl, blend the cookie crumbs, ground nuts, and melted margarine. Transfer to the prepared pan and press the crumb mixture onto the bottom and sides of the pan. Bake 5 minutes, then allow to cool. In a large bowl combine the tofu "ice cream," peanut butter, and honey, mixing until well blended. Spoon into the prepared crust. Freeze several hours or overnight.

Before serving, bring the pie to room temperature for 5 minutes, carefully remove the sides from the pan, and sprinkle the chocolate curls or shavings over the top of the pie, along the outer edge.

*12 servings*

### Nutritional Analysis

| | | |
|---|---:|---|
| Kilocalories | 655 | Kc |
| Protein | 15.6 | Gm |
| from soy | 4.3 | Gm |
| Fat | 41 | Gm |
| Percent of calories from fat | 54 | % |
| Cholesterol | 0 | mg |
| Dietary fiber | 3 | Gm |
| Sodium | 590 | mg |
| Calcium | 23 | mg |

# Tofu Pumpkin Pie

*Try this version of a family favorite—you may start a new holiday tradition. The egg-replacing product is available in natural-food stores.*

*For Crust:*
- 1 cup unbleached all-purpose flour
- 1/8 teaspoon salt
- 1/2 cup (1 stick) soy margarine, cut into small pieces
- 2 tablespoons ice water

*For Filling:*
- 2 cups canned pumpkin purée
- 1 1/2 cups extra-firm silken tofu, drained and patted dry
- 1 cup sugar (or a natural sweetener)
  Energ-E Egg Replacer for 2 eggs
- 1 teaspoon vanilla extract
- 1 teaspoon ground cinnamon
- 1/2 teaspoon ground ginger
- 1/4 teaspoon ground nutmeg

To make the crust, combine the flour and salt in a food processor. Blend in the margarine with short pulses until the mixture becomes crumbly. With the machine running, add the 2 tablespoons water through the feed tube and blend until the dough just starts to hold together. Transfer the dough to a work surface and flatten to form a disc. Wrap in plastic and refrigerate while preparing the filling.

Preheat the oven to 375°F. To make the filling, in a food processor, combine the pumpkin and tofu until well blended. Add the sugar, Egg Replacer combined with water for

2 eggs, vanilla, cinnamon, ginger, and nutmeg, mixing until smooth and well combined.

On a lightly floured surface, roll out the dough to fit a 9-inch pie plate. Fit the dough into the pie plate and trim and flute the edges. Pour the filling into the crust, and bake for about 50 minutes, or until firm.

*8 servings*

| Nutritional Analysis | | |
| --- | --- | --- |
| Kilocalories | 314 | Kc |
| Protein | 7.6 | Gm |
|   from soy | 3.5 | Gm |
| Fat | 13 | Gm |
| Percent of calories from fat | 37 | % |
| Cholesterol | 0 | mg |
| Dietary fiber | 2 | Gm |
| Sodium | 215 | mg |
| Calcium | 50 | mg |

# Banana Walnut Bread

*For best results, be sure to use extra-ripe bananas, as they will be sweeter.*

1½    cups unbleached all-purpose flour
½    cup soy flour
1½    teaspoons baking powder
¼    teaspoon salt
2    ripe bananas, peeled and cut into chunks
½    cup vanilla soy milk
¼    cup safflower oil
½    cup sugar
½    cup soft tofu, drained and patted dry
1    teaspoon vanilla extract
½    cup chopped walnuts

Preheat the oven to 375 degrees. Lightly oil a 9 × 5-inch loaf pan and set aside. Sift the flours, baking powder, and salt into a large bowl and set aside. Place the bananas, soy milk, oil, sugar, tofu, and vanilla in a food processor and blend until smooth. Add the liquid ingredients to the dry ingredients and mix well. Fold in the chopped nuts. Fill the prepared pan with the batter and bake for 45 to 50 minutes, or until a toothpick inserted into the center comes out clean. Allow to cool in the pan before slicing.

*Makes 1 loaf (8 servings)*

## Nutritional Analysis

| | | |
|---|---:|---|
| Kilocalories | 298 | Kc |
| Protein | 8.7 | Gm |
| from soy | 4.2 | Gm |
| Fat | 13 | Gm |
| Percent of calories from fat | 38 | % |
| Cholesterol | 0 | mg |
| Dietary fiber | 3 | Gm |
| Sodium | 78 | mg |
| Calcium | 78 | mg |

# Blueberry Cheesecake

*Change the topping to suit your own taste, or serve this creamy cheesecake plain, if you prefer.*

    2   cups graham-cracker crumbs
    2   tablespoons soy margarine, melted
  2³/₄  cups firm silken tofu, drained and patted dry
   ¹/₂  cup soy milk
   ¹/₄  cup safflower oil
    1   tablespoon cornstarch
    1   teaspoon vanilla extract
  1¹/₂  cups fruit-sweetened blueberry spread
        (or blueberry pie filling)

Preheat the oven to 350 degrees. Lightly oil a 9-inch springform pan, or coat with nonstick cooking spray. Place the crumbs in the bottom of the springform pan, add the melted margarine, and toss with a fork until blended. Press the crumb mixture onto the bottom and sides of the pan, and bake for 5 minutes. Set aside. Combine the tofu, soy milk, oil, cornstarch, and vanilla in a food processor, and blend until smooth. Pour the filling into the prepared crust and bake for 30 minutes, or until firm. Remove from the oven and allow to come to room temperature. Place the blueberry topping in a small bowl and stir until smooth. Spread on top of the cheesecake and refrigerate several hours to chill before serving.

*8 servings*

## Nutritional Analysis

| | | |
|---|---:|---|
| Kilocalories | 321 | Kc |
| Protein | 8.7 | Gm |
| from soy | 6.0 | Gm |
| Fat | 15 | Gm |
| Percent of calories from fat | 41 | % |
| Cholesterol | 0 | mg |
| Dietary fiber | 2 | Gm |
| Sodium | 314 | mg |
| Calcium | 51 | mg |

# Chocolate–Banana Cheesecake

*Bananas and chocolate are a winning combination in this deca-dently rich cheesecake.*

*For Crust:*
- 2 cups graham-cracker crumbs
- 2 tablespoons soy margarine, melted

*For Filling:*
- 2 cups firm silken tofu
- 2 ripe bananas, peeled and cut into chunks
- 1/3 cup sugar (or a natural sweetener)
- 2 tablespoons soy margarine, at room temperature
- 2 teaspoons fresh lemon juice
- 1 teaspoon vanilla extract
- 2 ounces tofu chocolate

Preheat the oven to 350 degrees. Lightly oil a 9-inch spring-form pan or coat with nonstick spray and set aside. Place the crumbs directly in the pan, add the melted margarine, and toss with a fork to combine. Press the crumb mixture onto the bottom and sides of the pan, and bake for 5 minutes. Remove from the oven and set aside. Meanwhile, in a food processor, combine the tofu, bananas, sugar, margarine, lemon juice, and vanilla, and mix until well blended. Spread the filling evenly into the crust. Melt the tofu chocolate in a double boiler or a small saucepan over a larger saucepan of simmering water. Pour the melted chocolate into the filling and swirl with a thin spatula or knife to create a light and dark swirled pattern in the cake. Bake for 30 minutes, or until firm. Cool to room temperature. Refrigerate several hours to chill before serving.

*8 servings*

### Nutritional Analysis

| | | |
|---|---:|---|
| Kilocalories | 291 | Kc |
| Protein | 6.6 | Gm |
| from soy | 3.5 | Gm |
| Fat | 10 | Gm |
| Percent of calories from fat | 34 | % |
| Cholesterol | 0 | mg |
| Dietary fiber | 1 | Gm |
| Sodium | 272 | mg |
| Calcium | 46 | mg |

# CHAPTER EIGHT

# Shakes and More

There's no need to cross milkshakes off your list just because you need to lower your cholesterol levels. Vanilla, chocolate, strawberry, and everything in between, can still be yours to enjoy. Just combine soy milk, a scoop of soy protein powder, and some fruit, and you'll be on your way to downing nearly 20 grams of soy protein.

Try the shakes for breakfast, lunch, or a between-meal snack. Enjoy one as a reward for making a commitment to a healthier lifestyle. And don't forget to try the Hot Cocoa with Tofu Whipped Cream.

# Just Peachy Breakfast Shake

*Make this shake in the summer when sweet, fresh peaches are in season, or substitute a cup of your favorite fruit. Soy protein powders are available at natural-food stores.*

|   |   |
|---|---|
| 2 | fresh peaches, peeled and halved |
| 1 | tablespoon peach preserves |
| 1/2 | teaspoon vanilla extract |
| 1 | scoop soy protein powder |
| 1 | cup chilled soy milk |

Combine the peaches, preserves, and vanilla extract in a blender and blend until well combined, about 30 seconds. Add the soy protein powder and soy milk, and blend until thick and smooth, about 30 seconds longer.

*1 serving*

### Nutritional Analysis

| | | |
|---|---|---|
| Kilocalories | 294 | Kc |
| Protein | 26.1 | Gm |
| from soy | 24.8 | Gm |
| Fat | 5 | Gm |
| Percent of calories from fat | 14 | % |
| Cholesterol | 0 | mg |
| Dietary fiber | 13 | Gm |
| Sodium | 306 | mg |
| Calcium | 102 | mg |

# Strawberry Breakfast Shake

*Loaded with nutrients, this shake is a great way to start the day.
Using frozen fruit makes a thicker shake.*

> 1/2 cup soft silken tofu
> 1 tablespoon honey or strawberry jam
> 1 scoop soy protein powder
> 1 cup chilled soy milk
> 1 cup frozen fresh strawberries

Combine the tofu, honey, soy powder, and soy milk in a
blender and blend until smooth, about 30 seconds. Add the
frozen strawberries and blend until thick and creamy, about
30 seconds longer.

*1 serving*

| Nutritional Analysis | | |
|---|---:|---|
| Kilocalories | 342 | Kc |
| Protein | 31.6 | Gm |
|   from soy | 30.9 | Gm |
| Fat | 9 | Gm |
| Percent of calories from fat | 20 | % |
| Cholesterol | 0 | mg |
| Dietary fiber | 13 | Gm |
| Sodium | 315 | mg |
| Calcium | 152 | mg |

# Banana Split Shake

*A favorite dessert transformed into a luscious and healthful shake.*

1    ripe banana, peeled and cut into chunks
1/2  cup pineapple juice
1/2  cup chocolate or carob soy milk
1    scoop soy protein powder
1/2  cup vanilla tofu "ice cream"
1    whole strawberry (optional garnish)

In a blender, combine the banana, pineapple juice, soy milk, and soy powder and process until well blended. Add the tofu "ice cream" and blend until thick and smooth. Pour into a large glass and garnish with a whole strawberry, if desired.

*1 serving*

| Nutritional Analysis | | |
|---|---:|---|
| Kilocalories | 523 | Kc |
| Protein | 24.8 | Gm |
| from soy | 23.2 | Gm |
| Fat | 15 | Gm |
| Percent of calories from fat | 23 | % |
| Cholesterol | 0 | mg |
| Dietary fiber | 11 | Gm |
| Sodium | 527 | mg |
| Calcium | 258 | mg |

# Tropical Shake

1/2  cup fresh or canned mango chunks
1/2  cup pineapple juice
1/2  cup soy milk
1  scoop soy protein powder
1  ripe banana, peeled, cut into chunks, and frozen
    Small pineapple wedge or whole strawberry
       (optional garnish)

In a blender, combine the mango, pineapple juice, soy milk, and soy powder and blend until smooth. Add the frozen banana and blend until thick and creamy, about 30 seconds. To serve, pour into a tall glass and garnish with fresh fruit, if desired.

*1 serving*

| Nutritional Analysis | | |
| --- | --- | --- |
| Kilocalories | 367 | Kc |
| Protein | 23.6 | Gm |
| from soy | 21.5 | Gm |
| Fat | 4 | Gm |
| Percent of calories from fat | 7 | % |
| Cholesterol | 0 | mg |
| Dietary fiber | 13 | Gm |
| Sodium | 294 | mg |
| Calcium | 124 | mg |

# Berry Delicious Shake

*Frozen blueberries may be substituted for the frozen strawberries for a delicious, and decidedly purple, alternative.*

| | |
|---|---|
| ¹/₂ | cup cranberry juice |
| ¹/₂ | cup hulled fresh strawberries |
| 1 | cup vanilla soy milk |
| 1 | scoop soy protein powder |
| 1 | tablespoon raspberry jam |
| ¹/₂ | cup frozen strawberries |

Combine the cranberry juice, fresh strawberries, soy milk, soy powder, and jam in a blender and blend until smooth. Add the frozen strawberries and blend for 30 seconds or until thick and creamy. Pour into a large glass to serve.

*1 serving*

### Nutritional Analysis

| | | |
|---|---|---|
| Kilocalories | 373 | Kc |
| Protein | 25.0 | Gm |
| from soy | 24.2 | Gm |
| Fat | 6 | Gm |
| Percent of calories from fat | 13 | % |
| Cholesterol | 0 | mg |
| Dietary fiber | 10 | Gm |
| Sodium | 437 | mg |
| Calcium | 409 | mg |

# Mocha Shake

*The popular combination of coffee and chocolate makes this shake a favorite.*

> 1   cup chocolate or carob soy milk
> 1/2  cup strong coffee
> 1   scoop soy protein powder
> 1/2  cup chocolate or carob tofu "ice cream"

Place the soy milk, coffee, and soy powder in a blender and blend until smooth, about 30 seconds. Add the tofu "ice cream" and blend until thick. Pour into a large glass to serve.

*1 serving*

| Nutritional Analysis | | |
| --- | --- | --- |
| Kilocalories | 421 | Kc |
| Protein | 27.3 | Gm |
| from soy | 27.2 | Gm |
| Fat | 16 | Gm |
| Percent of calories from fat | 33 | % |
| Cholesterol | 0 | mg |
| Dietary fiber | 10 | Gm |
| Sodium | 537 | mg |
| Calcium | 382 | mg |

# Orange Delight

*Reminiscent of a favorite childhood ice cream bar, this shake is simply delightful.*

|       |                                |
|-------|--------------------------------|
| 1     | cup vanilla soy milk           |
| 1/3   | cup orange juice concentrate   |
| 1     | scoop soy protein powder       |
| 1/2   | teaspoon vanilla extract       |
| 1/2   | cup vanilla tofu "ice cream"   |

Combine the soy milk, orange juice concentrate, soy powder, and vanilla extract in a blender and blend until smooth, about 30 seconds. Add the tofu "ice cream" and blend until thick, about 30 seconds longer.

*1 serving*

| Nutritional Analysis | | |
|---|---:|---|
| Kilocalories | 575 | Kc |
| Protein | 28.4 | Gm |
|   from soy | 26.2 | Gm |
| Fat | 17 | Gm |
| Percent of calories from fat | 25 | % |
| Cholesterol | 0 | mg |
| Dietary fiber | 10 | Gm |
| Sodium | 608 | mg |
| Calcium | 409 | mg |

# Soy Nog

*Finally, guilt-free eggnog! Loaded with flavor but no cholesterol.*

1 1/2  cups vanilla soy milk
1  scoop soy protein powder
1  teaspoon rum extract (optional)
1/8  teaspoon ground nutmeg
Pinch turmeric
1  cup vanilla tofu "ice cream"

Place all the ingredients, except the tofu "ice cream," in a blender and blend until smooth, about 30 seconds. Add the tofu "ice cream" and blend until thick and creamy, about 30 seconds. Serve in eggnog cups, and garnish with an extra dash of nutmeg, if desired.

*4 servings*

| Nutritional Analysis | | |
| --- | --- | --- |
| Kilocalories | 171 | Kc |
| Protein | 7.8 | Gm |
| from soy | 7.8 | Gm |
| Fat | 7 | Gm |
| Percent of calories from fat | 38 | % |
| Cholesterol | 0 | mg |
| Dietary fiber | 3 | Gm |
| Sodium | 219 | mg |
| Calcium | 133 | mg |

# Hot Cocoa

*A sweet indulgence that can soothe the soul while it adds several grams of soy protein to your day.*

| | |
|---|---|
| 2 | cups soy milk |
| 2 | tablespoons cocoa or carob powder |
| 1 | scoop soy protein powder |
| 1¹/₂ | tablespoons sugar (or a natural sweetener) |
| 1 | teaspoon vanilla extract |

Combine all the ingredients in a blender and blend until smooth. Pour the mixture into a small saucepan and stir with a wire whisk over medium heat for 1 to 2 minutes, or until hot. Do not boil. Serve in cups or mugs.

*2 servings*

### Nutritional Analysis

| | | |
|---|---:|---|
| Kilocalories | 217 | Kc |
| Protein | 16.6 | Gm |
| from soy | 15.7 | Gm |
| Fat | 6 | Gm |
| Percent of calories from fat | 23 | % |
| Cholesterol | 0 | mg |
| Dietary fiber | 6 | Gm |
| Sodium | 258 | mg |
| Calcium | 95 | mg |

# CHAPTER NINE

# Sample Menus

The sample menus in this chapter are designed primarily to answer the question: "How can I maximize the soy-protein content in any meal of the day?" In this chapter, several menu suggestions are given for breakfast, lunch, and dinner that show how to maximize soy protein content. They are meant to be used as guidelines to help you plan your meals, and not as a "diet" to be rigidly adhered to. The menus illustrate that, by combining two or more soy-based recipes in one meal, you can actually fulfill the daily suggested soy protein requirements to reduce your cholesterol.

To customize menus that will fill your particular needs, you need to identify those of your meals where high-cholesterol foods are a problem. If you already eat a reasonably low cholesterol breakfast of toast and cereal, for example, then the only change you may need to make is to switch from dairy milk to soy milk on your cereal.

Similarly, if your lunches generally lean toward the soup

and salad end of the spectrum, rather than bacon cheese-burgers and milkshakes, then you may need to concentrate more of your efforts on making changes at dinner.

On days when you are unable to prepare a soy protein–based meal, try to have at least one soy shake, and maybe a handful of roasted soy "nuts" as a snack.

While some menus are relatively low in calories, there are others that are decidedly "hearty." You decide what combination is best for your needs. The primary purpose of the recipes in this book is to provide you with great-tasting meal suggestions that will increase your soy protein intake and help to reduce your cholesterol.

The grams of protein listed at the end of each sample menu are calculated for a single serving. Menu items that are given in this book are listed in **bold**, followed by the page number where the recipe can be found.

# BREAKFAST MENUS

Enjoy these breakfasts with your favorite coffee, tea, or juice.

**Strawberry Breakfast Shake** (page 167)
Toasted bagel
**Tofruitti Bagel Spread** (page 47;) (35.3 gms soy protein)

Hot or cold cereal with 4 oz. soy milk
Choice of toast, bagel, or English muffin
**Tofu Breakfast Spread** (page 49;) (6.0 gms soy protein)

**Tofu Pancakes** (page 37)
Soy sausage (4 oz) (24.3 gms soy protein)

**French Toast** (page 39)
**Tempeh Bacon** (page 45) (28.0 gms soy protein)

**Scrambled Tofu with Sautéed Vegetables** (page 29)
Toast with **Miso Tahini Spread** (page 51)
(12.9 gms soy protein)

**Mushroom "Cheese" Omelet** (page 31)
Bagel with **Tofu Breakfast Spread** (page 49)
(13.9 gms soy protein)

**Scrambled Tofu with Soy Sausage and Peppers** (page 33)
Toast with apple butter (13.1 gms soy protein)

# LUNCH MENUS

Vary the sandwich breads according to your taste. Mix and match the soups and sandwiches. Add a favorite beverage and, if you're still hungry, enjoy a bit of dessert.

**Creamy Vegetable Soup** (page 53)
**"No Egg" Salad** sandwich (page 59) (16.8 gms soy protein)

**Tofu Miso Soup** (page 57)
Grilled soy cheese sandwich (1 oz. soy cheese)
(14.6 gms soy protein)

**Winter Vegetable Bisque** (page 55)
**Soy-Good Burger** (page 76) (14.8 gms soy protein)

Tossed Salad with **Creamy Herb Dressing** (page 86)
**Spicy Soy Chili** (page 70) (15.6 gms soy protein)

**Composed Salad Platter** (page 84)
**Almost-Instant Chocolate Mousse** (page 145)
(49.8 gms soy protein)

**Creamy Vegetable Soup** (page 53)
**Sloppy Joes** (page 68) (7.1 gms soy protein)

**Tofu Miso Soup** (page 57)
**Tofu-Tahini Sandwich Spread** sandwich (page 90)
**Blueberry Cheesecake** (page 161) (15.4 gms soy protein)

# DINNER MENUS

Whether cooking for yourself, or family and friends, these menus are sure to please. When guests are coming, add some wine and a loaf of warm bread to create a special meal.

Salad with **Creamy Mustard Dressing** (page 88)
**Jambalaya** (page 124)
Rice
**Chocolate-Banana Cheesecake** (page 163)
(23.2 gms soy protein)

**Tofu Cutlets with Creamy Mushroom Sauce** (page 136)
Broccoli and carrots
New potatoes
**Peaches and "Cream" Pie** (page 153) (17.6 gms soy protein)

**Tofu Miso Soup** (page 57)
**Ginger Tempeh Stir-Fry** (page 103)
Rice
**Almost-Instant Chocolate Mousse** (page 145)
(37 gms soy protein)

Mixed greens salad with **Creamy Herb Dressing** (page 86)
**Tofu Lasagna** (page 93)
**Fresh Strawberry Pudding** (page 148)
(29.6 gms soy protein)

**Tofu Stroganoff** (page 121)
Noodles
Steamed zucchini and carrots
**Fresh Fruit with Creamy Lemon Sauce** (page 143)
(18.4 gms soy protein)

**Creamy Vegetable Soup** (page 53)
**Curried Tofu** (page 132)
Rice
**Pineapple-Almond Bread Pudding** (page 149)
(23.1 gms soy protein)

**Salad of Mixed Greens with Creamy Mustard Dressing**
(page 88)
**Spinach-Stuffed Pasta Shells with Cream Sauce** (page 138)
**Banana Walnut Bread** (page 159) (29.6 gms soy protein)

**No-Meat Loaf** (page 105)
Roasted potatoes and carrots
Steamed green beans
**Peanut Butter Pie** (page 155) (31.4 gms soy protein)

**Tempeh Cutlets with Creamy Mustard Sauce** (page 115)
Mashed potatoes
Steamed spinach
**Tofu Pumpkin Pie** (page 157) (26.9 gms soy protein)

# GLOSSARY

**Egg Replacer:** A product made by Ener-G Foods, Inc., and sold in natural-food stores. Made mostly from potato starch. When combined with water, it can be used to replace eggs, especially in baking.

**Gomasio:** A condiment made by grinding together roasted sesame seeds and sea salt. Also called sesame salt, gomasio is a delicious alternative to grated parmesan cheese.

**Miso:** A fermented soybean paste, which is used in soups, sauces, and as a seasoning. Made from soybeans combined with rice, barley or other ingredients, miso is rich in protein, and is known for its many health benefits, when used on a regular basis. Miso paste comes in several varieties, from the mellow and mild white miso to the stronger and more robust red miso.

**Soy Flour:** Soybeans that have been ground into flour for use in baking. Since soy flour has no gluten, it creates a heavy bread and therefore should be combined with other flours in a recipe.

**Soy Milk:** A beverage made from ground soybeans and

water that can be used to replace dairy milk for drinking, cooking, and baking. It is available plain or flavored, and comes in regular and low-fat varieties.

**Soy Cheese:** A soy-based alternative to dairy cheese that is available in several varieties, including mozzarella, cheddar, and parmesan.

**Soy Protein Powder:** Any of several commercially prepared protein supplements that come in powdered form that are combined with fruit juice or soy milk to make high-protein shakes.

**Soy Sauce:** A condiment, made from fermented soybeans, that is often high in sodium and can contain additives. (See Tamari Soy Sauce.)

**Tamari Soy Sauce:** A high-quality, naturally fermented soy sauce, made from soybeans, wheat, and sea salt. Wheat-free and low-sodium varieties of tamari are also available at natural-foods stores.

**Tempeh:** Cooked cultured soybeans that have been pressed into cakes. Tempeh has a dense "meat-like" texture that lends itself to grilling and sautéing. It is also used in stir-fries, stews, and casseroles, and can be grated and used to replace ground meat.

**Textured Soy Protein:** Also called textured vegetable protein, or TVP, this is a dry product that, when rehydrated, resembles ground meat. It's best when used to make chili, tacos, sloppy joes, or spaghetti sauce.

**Tofu:** Soybean curd made by combining soy milk with a coagulant. Called "meat without the bone" in China, tofu is available in two varieties: regular, or Chinese, and silken, or Japanese. Both of these varieties come in a range of textures, from soft to extra-firm. The regular firm varieties are perfect for sautéing and stir-frying, while the silken and softer versions can be used to replace soft cheeses in everything from lasagna to cheesecake.

# INDEX